Fog On The Hill

General Gage Here We Are Come Get Us
The Battle of Bunker Hill

To: Deb,
Enjoy our history!
all the best,
Marc

Marc Stockwell-Moniz

Fog On The Hill
General Gage Here We Are Come Get Us
The Battle of Bunker Hill

Edited by Haley North

Book Cover: Etching of British Lt. General Thomas Gage

Military Governor Massachusetts Bay 1774-1775 and the King's Colors of 1707

Summary: The epic story of the Battle of Bunker Hill fought on June 17, 1775

Vox audita perit littera scripta manet

This book is dedicated to the eminent historian Mr. Thomas Fleming. It was Mr. Fleming who renewed the relevance and interest in the epic and grand story of the Battle of Bunker Hill. I will forever be grateful to Mr. Fleming for always having time for me.

The spoken word perishes, but the written word remains.

Fog On The Hill
General Gage Here We Are Come Get Us
The Battle of Bunker Hill

Table of Contents

Fog On The Hill
General Gage Here We Are Come Get Us
The Battle of Bunker Hill

Introduction

It was nearly two and one-half centuries ago in April of 1775, that thousands of ordinary men from New England mustered in Cambridge, Massachusetts. The beautiful spring-days unfortunately held the specter of war with Britain because of the recent Battle of Lexington and Concord.

Cambridge was a lovely town, however each American militiaman had a much better place to be. Until some unknown time in the future, these American patriots would be separated from their families. They would be separated from their livelihoods. The men gathered in Cambridge because of American ideals. These ideals demanded and called for them to be present, during this grave and perilous time. Liberty and freedom called. Unalienable rights and democracy called. Opportunity and equality called.

The tensions between the British government and its American colonies began in 1768, with the advent of the Townsend Acts. British troops were sent to Boston to quell the rancorous population. The mixture of British troops and the implacable Bostonian population would eventually lead to major troubles.

Ordinary British men conscripted mostly from the lower classes of British society, were ordered to Boston by their monarch and the British ruling class. This ruling class was an aristocratic hierarchy. It was led by King George III, Prime Minister Lord Frederick North, the British Parliament and high-ranking military officers. This foreign, menacing and occupying-army in Boston was truly an ominous force. It was a clear and imminent threat to the welfare of the people of Massachusetts. The people of Massachusetts and all of New England knew why the king's troops were occupying Boston. The population understood what was expected of this army. It would become nothing but trouble for them.

Whether one was a loyalist or a patriot, clear boundaries were drawn by each side. Everybody in Massachusetts joined one or the other faction. Tragically, the prospect of more bloodshed was very high.

By mid-June 1775, the British Redcoats in Boston were surrounded and consequently were in distress from the robust patriot-siege. Recently, the British Army had taken an inglorious beating on April 19, 1775, by these same American farmers and shop keepers. The time was becoming quite late for the vaunted British Army. The Siege of Boston was about to enter its third month in just a few days and the British desperately needed end this humiliating blockade.

All signs suggested something terrible was about to happen again. Most of the people of Massachusetts no longer recognized Military Governor General Thomas Gage's authority and his legitimacy to rule Massachusetts. The British needed to break loose from the Siege of Boston and reassert their dominance over these new world feisty-upstarts. They needed to breakout of Boston and regain their political authority. The British simply had no choice. But could they do it?

In a century and one-half, the majority British population of colonial America was morphing into Americans. These new world people started to talk with a different accent. They enjoyed new found freedoms and self-rule. There were endless opportunities for all. While the Americans treasured their ancestral roots of English, Scottish, Welsh, Irish, Dutch, German and African origins, there was little doubt that a new population was emerging. It's easy to understand why the colonial people of Boston began to think of themselves as separate from the British people. The occupying British Army certainly recognized these differences and were quick to remind the colonials of this fact. These differences accumulated over several generations and were now more apparent than ever before. A political separation was possible. Everything was uncertain. The American people would soon offer an answer to a possible political separation.

The Battle of Bunker Hill, by Howard Pile, 1897

Fog On The Hill

General Gage Here We Are Come Get Us
The Battle of Bunker Hill

Part One: The Time Has Arrived to Leave the Empire

Orders Are Issued to Fortify Charlestown

On April 19, 1775, the British Army occupied Bunker Hill and the Charlestown Peninsula. Lieutenant General Thomas Gage, the Military Governor of Massachusetts Bay, didn't order his troops to Charlestown, it was only by default that 1,500 British Army Regulars were there. The Redcoats resting on Bunker Hill were trying to recuperate from their day-long fiasco. They had fought all day on the battle road coming back from Lexington and Concord. General Gage's troops were weary and beaten from battling nearly 4,000 Massachusetts militiamen. The Redcoats were laying on the ground exhausted. The troops slept on Bunker Hill that night.

The following day General Gage ordered all of his troops off the Charlestown Peninsula back to Boston. The lack of insight by General Gage to hold the high ground in Charlestown was a major blunder. The fog of war had just introduced itself to the British Army.

Two months later on June 15, 1775, thousands of New England militiamen were bivouacked in the American camp located in Cambridge, Massachusetts. They were carrying out their solemn duty in the Siege of Boston. These patriots were settling down for another routine day of brief military drills and boredom. A handful of men walked the length of the camp selling liquor and vegetables. Even in this time of danger and economic uncertainty, commerce still managed to prevail among some of the more enterprising militiamen.

On this same day, a document of great magnitude was issued by the Massachusetts Committee of Safety. The Committee of Safety was meeting at General Artemus Ward's headquarters. This edict would soon affect the lives of the gathered American militiamen forever. For some of them their time would be short.

The Committee of Safety Document Reads As Follows:

"Whereas, it appears of Importance to the Safety of this Colony, that possession of the Hill, called Bunkers' Hill, in Charlestown, be securely kept and defended; and also, some one hill or hills on Dorchester Neck be likewise Secured. Therefore, Resolved, Unanimously, that it be recommended to the Council of War, that the abovementioned Bunker's Hill be maintained, by sufficient force being posted there; and as the particular situation of Dorchester Neck is unknown to this Committee, they advise that the Council of War take and pursue such steps respecting the Same, as to them shall appear to be for the Security of this Colony." (1)

Within a day and one-half of this decree, American militiamen led by Colonel William Prescott were in Charlestown building an earthen redoubt on a small hill. Certain parts of this small hill were occasionally known as Russell's Pasture, Green's Pasture or Breed's Pasture. This smaller hill, in the southeast corner of Charlestown is actually an "extension" of the adjacent and larger 110-foot Bunker Hill. This small hill eventually came to be known as Breed's Hill. It rises 65 feet-high and is logistically very close to Boston. Both of these hills overlooked the besieged colonial-town of Boston. Boston and Charlestown are separated only by the mouth of the Charles River.

Historical Accuracy of the Name of the Battle of Bunker Hill

It's important to clarify the confusion where the epic Battle of Bunker Hill was fought in Charlestown. Some bewilderment of the crucial fighting areas still exists even today.

While Bunker Hill was listed in the Charlestown deeds and town records for decades before 1775, the name Breed's Hill was not named in any official document until 1816. This confusion perhaps started with General James Wilkinson. Wilkinson wrote a description of the Battle of Bunker Hill in his book, *The War of Independence*. He referred to the battle as the Battle of Breed's Hill.

Years after the Battle of Bunker Hill, some confusion of its name began to manifest itself. Eventually historians specified the area where the redoubt had been built and called this area Breed's Hill. This recognition was to distinguish it from Bunker Hill. Prescott's Redoubt was not located in farmer Ebeneezer Breed's Pasture. It was actually located in Russell's Pasture, which was several-hundred feet away from Ebeneezer Breed's land. Prescott's Redoubt was built on what today is known as Breed's Hill.

This fact is worthy of notice because it enables us to account for some of the disputes which have been attached to the names of the well-known fighting areas of the battle. The New Hampshire Regiments of Colonel John Stark and Colonel James Reed, along with Captain Thomas Knowlton and his Connecticut men, were fighting fiercely behind the rail fence at the base of Bunker Hill. The British assault at the rail fence was a major aspect of the battle, as was the fighting on the Mystic River beach. The fight at the rail fence, along with the ensuing assault by British Regulars up the slopes of Bunker Hill, justifies the name of the battle as the Battle of Bunker Hill. This is where a significant amount of the Battle of Bunker Hill was fought. As the reader knows, orders were issued by the Committee of Safety to fortify Bunker Hill and not Breed's Hill. These facts are absolute. A large portion of the battle was fought on Breed's Hill. A significant portion of the battle was fought at Prescott's Redoubt and the surrounding sloping-topography. Leading down the gentle slopes of Breed's Hill to the town of Charlestown is also where some of the battle was fought. The Americans were flanking the British advances in Charlestown and all along the southern-slopes of Breed's Hill.

(**Author's Note:** It is worthy to recognize that the British landing in Charlestown on June 17, 1775, has been referred to as both Moulton's Point or Morton's Point. The author has chosen to use Moulton's Point.) Currently, there is a small historical-marker mounted on the outside wall of a building in the Charlestown Naval Yard which proclaims the following:

The Battle of Bunker Hill
17 June 1775
This tablet marks the general position of Moulton's Point where
the British troops landed and formed for the first assault.

The Worcester County Convention and the Political Genesis of American Independence and Self-Rule

The Massachusetts Bay Government Act was passed by the British Parliament on May 20, 1774. This act abrogated the existing 1691 colonial charter of Massachusetts Bay. This act was one of the Intolerable Acts, also known as the Repressive Acts or the Coercive Acts. Included in this edict, a military governor would be appointed to suppress dissent and restore order in Massachusetts Bay. However, the people of one particular Massachusetts county had better plans and ideas for themselves and they rapidly proceeded forward. The people of Worcester County decided that they would simply free themselves of British rule and no longer be subordinate to Parliament as British subjects.

Enter the Worcester County Convention of 1774.

August 9, 1774, the Worcester County Convention convened. By September 6, 1774, its leadership had asked that all the militia officers in the county to resign. This rebellious act fundamentally purged the militia leadership of any remaining Tory officers. At least half of the colonels prior to the convention were known to have loyalist sympathies. Patriot men were then elected in their stead and given command. The other ten counties of Massachusetts Bay quickly followed Worcester County's lead.

The result of the Worcester County Convention was that the population no longer recognized the British government as the legal political authority inside Massachusetts. Outside the occupied town of Boston, the people of Massachusetts stopped cooperating with any aspect of British rule. The people of Massachusetts simply started to rule themselves sans the British Parliament. They were now conducting their governmental affairs as citizens of the free state of Massachusetts. The people of Massachusetts deftly and peacefully dismissed British political rule.

The genesis of the Massachusetts Provincial Congress followed soon thereafter on October 7, 1774.

Americans Learn of the British Breakout Plans

A substantial number of patriot civilians remained inside Boston. They became a valuable asset to General Artemus Ward. They were literally the eyes and ears of the American leadership. They gathered valuable information regarding any British movement. On June 13, 1775, some of these patriots had overheard British officers talking about an impending breakout from the town. The British had planned to occupy Dorchester Heights. Oddly, this vital information first made its way to the New Hampshire Committee of Safety and then quickly back south via an express rider to the Massachusetts Committee of Safety. Within minutes of the arrival of the express rider, this important news had reached General Artemus Ward's headquarters. The Americans had learned that General Thomas Gage was preparing to occupy Dorchester Heights on the night of June 18, 1775. Dorchester Heights was the first objective of the British. Once Dorchester Heights was secured; the British would attempt to march into Cambridge to scatter the Americans. The British would also land on the

Charlestown Peninsula using waterborne troops. From Charlestown the British would march to Cambridge. Simultaneously, the British would converge on Cambridge from opposite sides of the town.

The Commanding American and British Generals

Commanding the New England forces was forty-seven-year-old Major General Artemus Ward. After learning of the news of the Battle of Lexington and Concord, General Ward got up from his sick bed and rode to Cambridge. He took command of the American troops on April 20, 1775.

Artemus Ward was born in Shrewsbury, Massachusetts in 1727. General Ward was a veteran of the French and Indian War. He served under the British commander, Lt. Colonel Sir Robert Abercromby. General Artemus Ward was a descendant of the Massachusetts Pilgrims.

In England, Lieutenant General Thomas Gage was appointed as the Military Governor of Massachusetts Bay in early 1774. He was no stranger to America. He also fought in the French and Indian War and was married to American Margaret Kemble. General Gage was favorably inclined and fond toward Americans. General Gage had every intention of resolving the pressing issues regarding Britain's colonial subjects. It would not be easy. What the newly appointed governor wanted most of all was to simply divert a war with the Americans.

General Thomas Gage arrived in Boston in May of 1774, and was sent to Massachusetts to keep the peace and also to enforce the closure of the Port of Boston. The Boston Port Act was set to take effect on June 1, 1774. Naturally, no Bostonian was happy with its closing. The welfare of everybody depended upon the port. The British government was making a big mistake. Trouble quickly started to brew. Because of this situation, Boston and Massachusetts Bay would soon devolve into a terrible economic decline. Rapidly after several weeks it did just that. It was clear that the British government didn't care about the welfare of the town of Boston. But somehow General Thomas Gage was expected to make the best of a bad situation created by his own government.

General Gage had great empathy for the Americans. To his credit he would often listen to the complaints of the Bostonians. He was very lenient toward them. When a group of young boys complained to General Frederic Haldimand that their sleigh riding hill had been damaged, Haldimand ordered it to be repaired. When General Haldimand reported the boy's complaint to General Gage, he was reported to have sighed and said mournfully, "It is impossible to beat the notion of liberty out of these people. It is rooted in 'em from their childhood." (2)

When General Thomas Gage arrived in Boston, in May of 1774, he faced a stubborn populace unsure of the rapid turn of events. But even within the fledgling and early moments of the American Revolution; Americans were still very proud of their British ancestry and had cherished their role as British subjects in the British Empire. Many Americans were ambivalent about breaking free from British protection, its economy and the world of a powerful grand-empire. The colonists offered petitions and beseeched King George III and his Parliament to better understand their grievances. The colonists wanted to reach a legal and political resolution of their grievances. Americans considered the British Parliament as the villain in these troubled times, and not their beloved sovereign King George III. Americans felt certain that when King George III received their petition for reconciliation, he would rescue them from the tyrannical policies of Lord Frederick North and the British Parliament. Lamentably, the Americans were wrong in their naive assumptions regarding their monarch. Their effort fell upon deaf-ears.

Meanwhile in London, King George III and Prime Minister Lord Frederick North felt comfortable with the probability of war. Both men fully embraced the idea of an all-out war with the colonists. Both men believed that this rabble of new-world colonists had to be taught a lesson. King George III and Lord North were very willing and perhaps even anxious to dole out this lesson. The likelihood of heavy violence perpetrated against British subjects living nearly 3,000 miles across the Atlantic Ocean was not a concern for them. Both of these men, and many politicians sitting in the British Parliament, believed that the honor of the British Empire had to be preserved at all cost. This was a paramount belief.

There was a small contingent of politicians in Parliament who resisted the overtures of war against the Americans. Most notably of these politicians was Isaac Barre. Barre championed the American cause. He coined the phrase Sons of Liberty. Additionally, John Wilke supported the American rebels. Although their efforts amounted to token opposition to Lord North's aggressive policies, they warned Parliament about the possibility of military failure and the folly to suppress the ideals of the seeds of American liberty.

British troops continued to arrive in Boston in late 1774. By November 17, 1774, British forces had climbed to 11 regiments along with artillery.

Redcoats came from Quebec, New York and New Jersey and were feeling confidant and cocky. Outside of the Tory or loyalist civilians of Massachusetts, the British disdainfully looked down upon the American population. One British officer writes home on December 26, 1774:

"Our army is in high spirits; and at present this town is pretty quiet. We get plenty of provisions, cheap and good in their kind; we only regret that necessity obliges us to enrich, by purchasing from a set of people we would wish to deprive of so great an advantage."

Another officer, in a letter written only one month earlier, portrays the American people in this light.

"As to what you hear of their taking arms to resist the force of England, it is mere bullying, and will go no further than words; whenever it comes to blows, he that can run the fastest will think himself best off; believe me, any two regiments here ought to be decimated if they did not beat, in the field, the whole force of Massachusetts province; for though they are numerous they are but a mere mob, without order or discipline, and very awkward at handling their arms." (3)

General Lord Hugh Percy spoke sarcastically about the Americans in a letter when he said,

"The people here are the most designing, artful villains in the World. They have not the least idea of either Religion or morality. Bostonians are braggarts who talk too much and do little…are in general made up of rashness and timidity. Quick and violent in their determinations, they are fearful in the execution of them, unless, indeed they are quite certain of meeting little opposition and then, like all other cowards, they are cruel and tyrannical. To hear them talk, you would imagine that they would attack us and demolish us every night. And yet whenever we appear, they are frightened out of their wits."

This condescending British attitude projected toward the American population and its fighting men would change drastically in five short months.

American Battlefield Commanders, Officers and Dr. Joseph Warren

Major General Dr. Joseph Warren was born in Roxbury, Massachusetts on June 11, 1741. Dr. Joseph Warren was a widower and father of four children. He lost his wife Elizabeth Hooton in 1773 and by 1775, he was engaged to Mercy Scollay. Dr. Joseph Warren was a very popular physician, orator, politician and ardent patriot. Dr. Joseph Warren, along with

James Otis and Samuel Adams, helped lead the charge to remove British troops from Boston after the Boston Massacre in 1770.

Dr. Joseph Warren was the chief architect of the Suffolk Resolves. Released on September 9, 1774, this declaration rejected the Massachusetts Government Act and The Intolerable Acts. The Massachusetts Government Act was passed by the British Parliament on May 20, 1774. This act effectively abrogated the Massachusetts Bay Charter of 1691. It gave its royally appointed governor wide ranging powers. The Suffolk Resolves declared the Government Act, imposed upon the people of Boston, to be unconstitutional. The Intolerable Acts were punitive laws passed by the British Parliament in 1774, after the Boston Tea Party. Dr. Joseph Warren and his righteous Suffolk Resolves had urged the people of Massachusetts to form their own government, withhold taxes to the British Crown and recommended economic sanctions against Britain. Subsequently, the Massachusetts Provisional Congress was founded on October 5, 1774. The Suffolk Resolves encouraged the populace to arm themselves. The First Continental Congress endorsed the Suffolk Resolves after receiving them from the dependable express-rider and American-patriot Paul Revere.

Dr. Joseph Warren was eventually elected president of the Massachusetts Provincial Congress on April 23, 1775. He was also a leader of the Committee of Safety. Earlier the Provincial Congress had established the Committee of Safety on October 20, 1774, to oversee actions taken for the defense and safety of Massachusetts. The task of the Committee of Safety was to supervise the process of a military buildup and provided for the procurement and disbursement of arms, munitions and supplies. By the spring of 1775, Dr Joseph Warren was orchestrating virtually all the American political positions regarding Massachusetts. Despite all the animosity between Britain and the colonists, Dr. Joseph Warren still preferred to have peace with the mother country.

Major General Dr. Joseph Warren, along with firebrand Samuel Adams and John Hancock, were the most important revolutionary figures in Massachusetts. Major General Dr. Joseph Warren was a dedicated man engulfed in idealism and the patriot cause. Dr. Joseph Warren was one of the first major proponents to espouse American liberty, freedom and independence.

Included in the American camp was an impressive Massachusetts militia-officer by the name of Colonel William Prescott. He was born in

Groton, Massachusetts on February 20, 1720, and resided in Pepperell. He was married to Abigale Hale of Sutton.

Colonel William Prescott stood over six-feet tall and was a powerful man. He was also calm, strong-willed and commanding. Prescott was a veteran of King George's War and the French and Indian War. During the French and Indian War, Colonel Prescott was present when Louisbourg was captured in 1745. He had recently led his troops, in the running-battle against the British on April 19, 1775. Colonel Prescott was a very well-liked and respected officer. He would eventually lead the Massachusetts troops at the Battle of Bunker Hill. He was in command of the American redoubt on Breed's Hill.

Other high-ranking and influential officers from Massachusetts were; Major General John Thomas, Engineer Colonel Richard Gridley and Colonel John Whitcomb. Major General John Thomas was ordered to secure the Boston Neck, while Colonel Richard Gridley would march to Bunker Hill with Colonel Prescott. There were 26 regiments from Massachusetts that answered the call-to-arms including one artillery-regiment.

From the tiny colony of Rhode Island, their regiments were commanded by Colonel James Varnum, Colonel Daniel Hitchcock and Colonel Thomas Church. They served under the overall leadership of Brigadier General Nathanael Greene. General Nathanael Greene and his Rhode Island men were ordered to support Major General John Thomas at the Boston Neck. The brilliant General Nathanael Greene would eventually be appointed by General George Washington, in late 1780, as the Commander of American troops in the Southern Campaign.

The northern neighbor of Massachusetts Bay, the colony of New Hampshire sent seasoned warriors to Cambridge. The most prominent of them was Colonel John Stark. Colonel John Stark is credited with coining the motto of: "Live Free or Die." (4) Stark eventually retired from military service in 1783, as a major general in the Continental Army.

Along with Colonel Stark, there were three other colonels from New Hampshire; Paul Sargent, Enoch Poor and James Reed. Notable Captains were, Henry Dearborn and Reuben Dow. Captain Dow had marched with Colonel Prescott from Pepperell to Cambridge and was nominally under Colonel Prescott's command. Dow was severely wounded at the Battle of Bunker Hill. Captain Dow led the Hollis Company.

The Connecticut militia arrived in Cambridge led by the war veteran Major General Israel Putnam. Major General Israel Putnam was born on

January 7, 1718, in Danvers, Massachusetts. By the year 1740, he had moved to Pomfret, Connecticut. One legendary story about this fearless man is; as a young man Putnam crawled into a wolf's den and killed the animal because it had been terrorizing Putnam's town. Putnam was determined to end this problem. He did just that!

When news of the fighting, at Lexington and Concord, reached Putnam on April 20, 1775, the feisty Putnam was working at his farm in Brooklyn, Connecticut. Putnam immediately saddled his horse and called out the alarm to his militiamen. He then rode nonstop to Cambridge. The very next day on April 21, Putnam was attending a Council of War at General Ward's headquarters. Putnam was a true warrior having served with Rogers' Rangers in the French and Indian War. He was promoted often. He quickly rose through the ranks from private to colonel. One of the interesting notions which "Old Put" championed was that the American fighting man would stand his ground as long as his legs were covered and protected. He was the embodiment of a valorous soldier.

Additionally in the American camp and serving directly under General Israel Putnam were: Colonels David Wooster, Joseph Spencer, Benjamin Hinman, David Waterbury, Samuel Parsons and Captain Thomas Knowlton. Captain Knowlton would distinguish himself fighting at the rail fence during the Battle of Bunker Hill.

Ineffectual General Gage Creates A British Disaster

Since September 1, 1774, General Thomas Gage had been sending his troops into the Massachusetts countryside to various powder houses. General Gage wanted to secure any and all patriot armaments and gunpowder. On April 19, 1775, the expedition that General Gage sent to Lexington and Concord had other significant reasons. When General Gage was informed that the Americans had amazingly confiscated four cannons from a British armory in Boston, General Gage acted upon this information. He ordered his Redcoats to retrieve them. The Americans were purportedly hiding these cannons on the farm of Colonel James Barrett in Concord.

The march to Concord to find the cannons was the primary reason that General Gage sent his Redcoats out on April 19, 1775. In addition, two of the leading American patriots, John Hancock and Samuel Adams, were allegedly hiding in Lexington. Hancock and Adams were the only patriots who didn't receive a pardon for their political rebel-rousing. If Hancock and Adams were arrested, they would have been executed by hanging.

Capturing and executing Hancock and Adams would have been very beneficial to the British effort to squelch the American rebellion. The execution of Adams and Hancock would have been a lesson to any American rebel not to bear arms against the Crown. If all went as planned, General Gage would accomplish the dual objective of capturing both Hancock and Adams and retrieving the stolen cannons. Both mission objectives were extremely important to General Gage. General Gage probably never reported the missing cannons to his superiors in London. There are no records indicating that General Gage informed his superiors. He didn't want them to find out about his negligence. This would have been both politically and militarily disastrous to the military governor of Massachusetts.

General Gage's embarrassment, stemming from his negligence to protect the cannons, may have been the impetus for the start of the American Revolutionary War. The political and military implications of these missing cannons were quite apparent to General Gage. He understood the significance of this theft. Unlike muskets and gunpowder, that could be used for hunting, cannons could be used only in battle. The theft of these cannons was an unmistakable preparation for war. General Gage was frantic to secure them before his superiors found out about his inattention.

Ultimately, General Thomas Gage failed to retrieve the pilfered cannons or arrest John Hancock and Samuel Adams. The day was a humiliating disaster for him. (5)

Aftermath of April 19, 1775

On the evening of April 19, 1775, only a few hours after the Battle of Lexington and Concord; Americans now understood they were enemies of their mother country. New Englanders and the fledgling American nation would continue to fight for liberty and General Gage understood this stark reality. General Gage would continue to try and quash the rebellion. The time for a complete break from Britain had apparently arrived for the Americans. The decisive day was approaching. There would be no turning back. The Americans and British were now mortal enemies.

It was late in the day of April 19, 1775, as the battered and beaten British Regulars limped along the road back to Charlestown. They were seeking the protection of the British Navy moored in Boston Harbor. The Redcoats staggered across the Charlestown Neck and then struggled up a hill to rest under the shelter of the big-guns.

Redcoat stragglers had alarmed the local-populace of the British approach into Charlestown. As the tired army filed in from the Charlestown Neck, the Redcoats met streams of people pouring out. The British Regulars were no longer pursued, but they vented their rage by frightening women and children as they emptied their muskets. The soldiers called for drink at taverns and houses and encamped for the night on a place called Bunker Hill. (6)

Many British were wounded. These were the lucky ones. They were the survivors of the first battle of the American Revolutionary War. Scores of other British soldiers lay dead from the running-battle. The pride of the grand British Army had been decimated by the minutemen of Massachusetts. The British soldiers resting on Bunker Hill were dazed and defeated. However, these soldiers would have a second opportunity to spend time on Bunker Hill. The fog of war would demand their presence.

The next British visit to Bunker Hill would be on June 17, 1775, a mere two-months from their current hell. General Thomas Gage didn't have a clue what to do next. General Gage had his troops on Bunker Hill on April 19, 1775, but he lacked the insight to keep them there and fortify the hill. This would later be a costly and abysmal mistake. General Gage recalled all of his men back to the encircled town of Boston the following day. In Boston the British would attempt to recoup from their grave losses.

Following the British close behind, the Americans were cautious to stay out of range of British warships in the harbor. Quickly, the British Army in Charlestown and Boston were immediately surrounded by hostile Americans. The Americans were securing their positions and quickly building basic fortifications. Comprising a semicircular siege for several miles, the Americans stationed troops from Charlestown, along the whole of the Charles River shore to the Back-Bay area. The American patriots also set up a watch, at both the Charlestown Neck and the Boston Neck near Roxbury. The Boston Neck was the only road leading in and out of Boston. This road was a crucial choke-point for the Americans.

Many British officers and soldiers changed their tune regarding their individual and collective opinion of Americans. It was now apparent to the British that the Americans would fight to the death.

General Hugh Percy, son of the powerful Duke of Northumberland, changed his low opinion of the American militiamen when he opined after the Battle of Lexington and Concord. Percy said,

"Whoever looks upon them as an irregular mob will find himself much mistaken. For my part, I never believed, I confess, that they would have attacked the King's troops, or have had the perseverance I found in them yesterday. They have men amongst them who know very well what they are about. Nor are several of them void of a spirit of enthusiasm for many…they advanced to within 10 yards to fire at me and other officers tho' they were morally certain of being put to death themselves in an instant."

Siege Lines Established: A Public Relations Race to Avert War

Within a few days of the Battle of Lexington and Concord, General Artemus Ward had reinforced the entire siege line surrounding the town of Boston. By April 29, 1775, the Committee of Safety had called out to all the towns of Massachusetts to send their militia.

Militiamen from Essex and Middlesex counties were stationed along the entire shoreline of Chelsea. This territory included Pullen Point and all of Rumney Marsh (Revere). Patriot observers were also stationed on Boston's two largest Harbor Islands, Noddle's Island and Hog Island. The islands jutted-out from Chelsea and completed the left wing of the semi-circular American defenses. Colonel John Stark and his New Hampshire Regiment were stationed in Medford, known at the time as Mystic. Colonel James Reed of New Hampshire, was stationed near the Charlestown Neck. Finally, some patriot militiamen were camped along the Mystic River to prevent the British from attempting to float up the river with their gun barges. (7)

On the diplomatic front; an all-out effort was made by both the British and the Americans to sway public opinion seeking political support regarding the recent battle of April 19, 1775. It was crucial to inform those in power and perhaps even more importantly to inform the general public about their version of events. This was an eighteenth-century campaign of public relations. Savvy leaders on both sides, who truly wanted to avert a war, knew that it was imperative to put forth the effort to stop any more bloodshed.

For the American position, Dr. Joseph Warren made a desperate attempt to appeal to the sensibilities of British politicians and to the British people. Dr. Joseph Warren sent a letter to Britain on a fast schooner named *Quero*. The mission of the *Quero* was to beat General Gage's official report of the Battle of Lexington and Concord to the politicians in the halls of Parliament. General Gage needed his version of the April 19, 1775, fiasco to exonerate his terrible decision to march out of Boston. The *Quero* successfully arrived two weeks before General Gage's report arrived in London. Woefully, Dr. Warren's plea was dismissed by the British government.

Dr. Joseph Warren's letter sent to Britain said,

"We cannot think that the honour, wisdom and valour of the Britons will suffer them longer to be inactive spectators of measures in which they themselves are so deeply interested; measures pursued in opposition to the solemn protests of many noble Lords, and expressed sense of conspicuous Commoners, whose knowledge and virtue have long characterized them as some of the greatest men in the nation... We sincerely hope that the great Sovereign of the Universe, who hath so often appeared for the English nation, will support you in very rational and manly exertion with these Colonies, for saving it from ruin; and that in a constitutional connection with the Mother Country, we shall soon be altogether a free and happy people."

Dr. Joseph Warren's letter was profound and sincere. His letter was expeditiously dismissed by the British.

The American Camp Inside Cambridge

Meanwhile in Cambridge on April 20, 1775, General Artemus Ward had set up his headquarters in the home of Johnathan Hastings. Hastings was a steward of Harvard College. The Hastings house was adjacent to the school and to the Cambridge Common, also known as the Harvard Green. This is where the American militia would be encamped from April 1775, through March 1776, during the Siege of Boston. Militiamen were pouring into Cambridge from all around New England. Men from Massachusetts, Connecticut, Rhode Island and New Hampshire converged as a fighting force under their commanders.

Geographically the New England colonies were not separated by a vast number of miles, but some differences existed among them. Commonly, the American warriors shared their love of liberty and freedom, the English language, and attended church services every Sunday. Yet many of these men were reluctant and sometimes even balked from receiving orders from an officer of a different colony. This type of adverse attitude would later be a hindrance at the Battle of Bunker Hill. This hindrance disguised itself. It was the fog of war stealthily securing itself into the American camp.

The Americans Slyly Wait

The officers attending the Council of War, at General Ward's headquarters, were debating whether or not to fortify the important hills of Charlestown. The heights of Charlestown overlooked Boston. Colonel Prescott and General Putnam called for an immediate occupation of Bunker Hill. This motion was immediately seconded by Colonel Thomas Gardner. The always cautious General Artemus Ward and the prudent Dr. Joseph Warren, argued for patience and no occupation of the Charlestown Heights at this time. Ward and Warren simply overruled Prescott, Putnam, and Gardner. They appealed to them to not act in any hasty manner.

Eventually the "old-war-horse" General Putnam, without any direct orders, seemingly wanted to force this issue. He ordered his Connecticut militia to march to Charlestown on May 13, 1775. He paraded his men through the deserted roads of Charlestown and up and down Bunker Hill and Breed's Hill. He did this in plain view of a British warship that was moored close by in Boston Harbor and adjacent to the village. The British witnessed this act of American aggression, but at no time did the sailors on *HMS Somerset* with her 32 heavy-guns fire in anger. Putnam's troops also held back from firing their guns. Miraculously, both sides avoided battle and bloodshed that day. The Americans turned and saluted the warship and gave a loud "war-hoop" and they simply marched away over Breed's Hill and then Bunker Hill back to Cambridge.

Despite conducting his daring and foolish military-exercise, General Putnam gained vital knowledge of Charlestown. Putnam's brief excursion gave him the opportunity to familiarize himself with the topography of the land and the strategic importance of both Bunker Hill and Breed's Hill. "Old Put" most likely wanted to build fortifications on both hills after reconnoitering the terrain. In the early morning hours of June 17, 1775, the feisty Putnam would have his opportunity to try and persuade the other American battlefield-commanders to do just that.

American Camp Conditions Inside Cambridge

The American camp was in a state of flux. Men departed for home as new men arrived. Most of the militiamen were farmers, shopkeepers and mechanics. All of them eventually needed to attend to their farms, livelihoods and families. Since there were no enlistment contracts to sign, it was legally impossible to keep the men lawfully secured to a military life. This dire situation was becoming apparent to all. Everybody in camp knew that the Siege of Boston was not coming to a conclusion any time soon. Discipline was hard for the officers to enforce, especially among the type of men who possessed a fierce allegiance to liberty and freedom. The most disciplined contingent of men were General Putnam's Connecticut troops. Putnam kept them busy with an endless array of drills while building fortifications on the outskirts of the American camp.

The strength of the American forces in camp was initially: Connecticut 2,200 men, Rhode Island 1,000 men, New Hampshire 1,056 men and Massachusetts about 6,054 men, not including the territory of Maine which organized a regiment. The newspapers were calling this band of rebels the Grand American Army. Each colony supplied their own men; the New Hampshire troops first enlisted under the authority of Massachusetts and received their supplies by her. In total, General Ward had approximately, 10,310 New Englanders protecting the countryside.

Commander General Artemus Ward on April 24, 1775, wrote to the Provincial Congress of Massachusetts and said:

"Gentlemen, - My situation is such, that if I have not enlisting orders immediately, I shall be left alone. It is impossible to keep the men here, except something be done. I therefore pray that the plan may be completed, and handed to me this morning, that you, gentlemen of the Congress, issue orders for enlisting men.

I am, gentlemen, yours &c.,

A. Ward." (8)

On the Cambridge Common most of the men were living in tents. Some of the men built simple lean-to structures and the industrious built small huts. Pitifully some men lived out in the open around campfires. And some of the lucky men received rooms in the Harvard dormitories. The Christ Church was converted into living quarters. Also, the homes vacated by loyalist families became homes to officers and their staff.

The Cambridge Common was overflowing with American troops and within just a few weeks concerns over hygiene and squalor permeated the camp. These filthy conditions were not addressed properly until General George Washington took command of this nascent New England Army. General Washington arrived on July 3, 1775. It's truly a wonder that mass scale disease did not manifest itself in the American camp. If hygienic conditions had not improved, as it eventually did, perhaps disease might have destroyed the American camp. The American Revolution could have been extinguished right then and there. There was also a smallpox outbreak inside Boston. General Gage was very concerned and eager to evacuate any person with smallpox. The American leadership made sure that smallpox didn't make its way to Cambridge and to the troops. They would not allow anybody with smallpox to cross over the American lines. American authorities would place the sufferers of smallpox on a boat and sail them to Salem, Massachusetts. The two precarious years of 1775 and 1776, were bad years for this deadly smallpox outbreak inside Boston.

British Conditions Inside Boston

Conditions inside the town of Boston were ghastly for the British. The British rank-and-file soldiers were living in tents on the Boston Common. British officers were billeted in homes within the confines of the town. When patriot civilians left Boston, some British soldiers finally had a roof over their heads. Patriot civilian-homes became barracks for the king's troops, along with various business buildings.

The diet of the British soldier was dreadful. They lacked much of what is regarded as a nutritious diet. Salted pork was the mainstay of what they ate. Sometimes it was the only food item that they consumed in a day. Even before the Battle of Lexington and Concord took place, American farmers and peddlers, with fresh food for sale, had long disappeared from the road leading into Boston. To complicate the awful food shortage for the British, many of the men had their women, whether they were wives legal or impermanent, encamped with them. These civilians also needed to be fed. Additionally, there were children to be fed. Approximately, 250 extra mouths needed sustenance. Women received half rations and the children received quarter rations. Food was always scarce and expensive during the siege. Occasionally the British Navy captured a transport ship with some food provisions onboard. These food caches hardly accounted for the needs of the British troops and the civilian population. Also, the fishing industry had come to an abrupt halt. Hunger permeated the town. The situation was appalling inside Boston. Life was perilous inside this once thriving and resourceful seaport-town. To his credit, General Gage tried his best to make sure that everybody had something to eat.

The consumption of alcohol was also a pressing problem for General Gage. Most of the enlisted soldiers were often drunk, as rum was cheap and cost only one copper. Boredom was another cause for concern for the British officers. There was only so much drilling and training to do attempting to keep the rank-and-file busy and occupied with pertinent tasks.

Finally, General Gage Acts

On Sunday May 21, 1775, General Gage ordered 100 troops, in conjunction with Vice Admiral Samuel Graves and his Royal Navy to sail to Grape Island. Grape Island is less than 20 miles south from Boston. The British were attempting to acquire food and supplies. Some American loyalists had remained on Grape Island and they often made provisions available for sale to the British. Sometimes these loyalists just gave away their provisions for free. For General Gage this mission had the promise of a modicum of success.

After collecting some supplies, the Redcoats were discovered by the patriots and fired upon. They were then hastily chased from the area by a larger assemblage of militiamen who arrived at the scene. The British departed Grape Island with only a small amount of goods. Their effort was largely a failure. Lt. John Barker of the King's Own Regiment said,

"This was the most ridiculous expedition that was ever plan'd." (9)

Perhaps General Gage just needed to exert some muscle and exercise his troops. But the fact still remained that General Gage still desperately needed to access a much larger amount of food and supplies. The Harbor Islands directly adjacent to Boston might be the answer for him. Farms with livestock were on these islands. The Harbor Islands became his last local option to amass any large amount of food and supplies. General Gage ordered the islands to be secured.

Chelsea Creek Debacle

Meanwhile the steadfast Massachusetts Provincial Congress President Dr. Joseph Warren and the Massachusetts Committee of Safety were quite aware of the food shortage inside Boston and the plight of an exasperated General Gage. The Americans quickly made plans to confiscate the Harbor Island supplies before the British could occupy them.

Another week had passed and General Gage still hadn't made any attempt to take the provisions off either Hog Island or Noddle's Island. Eventually, 600 Americans occupied the islands and successfully raided all of the livestock and supplies off the islands on May 26, 1775. The slow response of General Gage to secure the Harbor Islands enabled the

Americans to remove, 411 sheep, 27 cattle, 6 horses, valuable supplies and stores of hay. General Gage finally ordered Vice Admiral Graves to land about 170 Royal Marines to counter the American troops. A small battled ensued that the Americans won. The British withdrew their troops back to their warships and sailed back to Boston.

The lack of any large-scale effort by General Gage to remove the live-stock from the Harbor Islands highlighted his obvious inability to make crucial and timely decisions. He continuously dawdled about and because of his procrastination his men continued to suffer.

The Battle of Chelsea Creek and the Harbor Islands was another humiliating defeat for the British in little more than one month. The Royal Navy had lost *HMS Diana,* two Royal Marines shot dead and several wounded. The loss of *HMS Diana*, commanded by Vice Admiral Graves' nephew Lt. Thomas Graves, was the first British naval-vessel to be captured and then sunk by American forces in the American Revolutionary War. *HMS Dianna* was forced onto the banks of Chelsea Creek, ransacked and then lit on fire by the Americans and destroyed.

The British gained nothing from the Battle of Chelsea Creek. General Gage, Vice Admiral Graves and the Royal Navy were again stymied by the upstart American military and that pesky fog of war.

British Fortify Positions Within Boston

General Gage had vital and crucial work to shore-up British security inside Boston. Strategically General Gage was now busy building and fortifying military-positions. From the only land access into Boston, General Gage fortified the Boston Neck with ten, twenty-four-pound guns. Inside Boston on Copp's Hill in the northeast, Barton's Point in the northwest and Fort Hill in the middle of the eastern side of the town, all of these batteries were strengthened and fortified. The large guns on top of Copp's Hill would later be involved in the Battle of Bunker Hill.

Despite General Gage's completed fortifications, Boston was still vulnerable to attack. His forts had secured the northern and eastern borders of Boston, while Vice Admiral Grave's warships commanded a majority of the coastline. But the whole western-side of Boston, in the area of the Boston Common and the foot of Beacon Hill, was wide open to attack. The Back-Bay waterline was so shallow that none of Admiral Grave's warships could anchor there to protect the town. And any night attack by the Americans, would surprise the Redcoats camped in their tents on

Boston Common. In order to command the western shore and also to quell a possible uprising in the town, General Gage erected a small defensive-work on Beacon Hill. Ultimately, the four main defensive-works, along with the Beacon Hill fort, were all that General Gage was able to accomplish before the Battle of Bunker Hill.

British Reinforcements Arrive

Lt. John Barker of the King's Own wrote on May 1, 1775:

"We are anxiously awaiting the arrival of the General Officers and Troops that are expected; we want to get out of this coop'd up situation. We coul'd now do that I suppose but the G--- [Gage] does not seem to want it; there's no guessing what he is at; Time will shew."

One day before the British defeat at the Battle of Chelsea Creek, the triumvirate of British generals finally landed in Boston. General William Howe, General Henry Clinton and General John Burgoyne arrived with reinforcements. Generals Howe, Clinton and Burgoyne would each have a role in the upcoming Battle of Bunker Hill. They were met with cheers at Long Wharf by the Tories of Boston. The Tories believed that somehow these three generals were the answer to the rebellious countryside that was full of dangerous yokels who controlled all the events.

The generals arrived on *HMS Cerebus*, May 25, 1775. The following appeared in newspapers:

"When the three generals, lately arrived, were going into Boston, they met a packet coming out, bound to this place, (Newport) when, we hear, General Burgoyne asked the skipper of the packet, "What news there was?" And being told that Boston was surrounded by 10,000 country people asked, "How many Regulars there were in Boston?" and being answered 5,000, cried out, with astonishment, "What! Ten thousand peasants keep five thousand king's troops shut up! Well, let *us* get in, and we'll soon find "elbow room." Hence this phrase, "elbow-room," was much used all through the revolution. General Burgoyne is designated by elbow-room in the satires of the time. It is said that he loved a joke and used to relate, after his Canada reverses, while a prisoner of war, he was received with great courtesy by the people of Boston. When he stepped from the Charlestown ferryboat, he was really annoyed when an old lady, perched on a shed above the crowd, cried out at the top of a shrill voice: "Make way, make way-the general's coming! Give him elbow-room!" (10)

General Burgoyne regarded the New England Army as merely a make-shift army. Burgoyne's assessment was true. This description is exactly what the American militia was at this time; it was a makeshift army. But he was wrong in his perception that Americans were cowardly mechanics, shopkeepers and farmers. Burgoyne was convinced that if the Americans were attacked, they would run off and the rebellion would be ended. Perhaps General Burgoyne would not have made those comments if he was present in Boston just five weeks earlier, on the day of April 19, 1775.

The three British Major Generals were mocked by the Americans with this doggerel.

"Behold the *Cerebus* the Atlantic plow, Her precious cargo-Burgoyne, Clinton, Howe. Bow, wow, wow!"

The Stalemate Continues and British Breakout Plans Conceived

Not long after their arrival in Boston; Generals Howe, Clinton and Burgoyne were suggesting that the occupation of Bunker Hill and Dorchester Heights was critical to the success of the British breakout-plan. For the three newly arrived British generals, it was obvious to them that a deployment of troops should quickly be made to secure these heights to protect Boston. From these two strategic positions, the British would be able to sally forth into the countryside once again. It must have been puzzling to the generals why General Gage didn't hold the high ground at Bunker Hill. As we know, he held the Charlestown Heights a mere five weeks earlier. The British would now have to attempt to take the hill again.

Nearly three weeks had passed since the arrival of the triumvirate of generals. General Gage finally had a plan. With the support of his reinforcements, he would breakout from Boston and occupy Dorchester Heights and Bunker Hill. The operation was planned for June 18, 1775. General Gage's plan, as previously noted, was discovered and relayed to the American camp.

General Artemus Ward and Dr. Joseph Warren immediately started to make war preparations.

Dr. Joseph Warren Appeals for the Safety of All Civilians

During the two months from April 19, 1775, until the Battle of Bunker Hill on June 17, 1775, there was a large exchange of civilians flowing into and out of Boston. Tories living outside of Boston were being harassed and sought the safety of crown-rule. Some were threatened with violence.

Many feared for their lives. Some supporters of King George III left Massachusetts altogether. In contrast, patriot civilians were trying to exit the town and often faced impediments in their quest to leave. Patriot civilians started their exodus out of Boston as early as April 20, 1775. Ironically the Tories inside Boston didn't support the movement of people wanting to leave. The Tory belief was that General Ward's men were much less likely to attack Boston or set it ablaze if patriot sympathizers remained inside the town. Tories made it difficult for patriot civilians to depart. This included verbal harassment and occasional violence.

Dr. Joseph Warren was concerned with all noncombatant civilians. He sought to protect all of them. He reached out to General Gage with a letter. It reads as follows:

"Sir:-The unhappy situation into which this colony is thrown gives the greatest uneasiness to every man who regards the welfare of the empire, or feels for the distresses of his fellow-men; but even now much may be done to alleviate those misfortunes which cannot be entirely remediated; and I think it of the utmost importance to us, that our conduct be such as that the contending parties may entirely rely upon the honor and integrity of each other for the punctual performance of any agreement that shall be made between them. Your Excellency, I believe, knows very well the part I have taken in public affairs: I ever scorned disguise. I think I have done my duty: some will think otherwise; but be assured, sir, as far as my influence goes, everything which can reasonably be required of us to do shall be done, and everything promised shall be religiously performed. I should now be very glad to know from you, sir, how many days you will allow the people in Boston for their removal. When I have received that information, I will repair to Congress, and hasten, as far as I am able, the issuing a proclamation. I beg leave to suggest, that the condition of admitting only thirty wagons at a time into the town appears to me to be very inconvenient, and will prevent the good effects of a proclamation intended to be issued for encouraging all wagoners to assist in removing the effects from Boston with all possible speed. If Your Excellency will be pleased to take the matter into consideration, and favor me, as soon as may be, with an answer, it will lay me under a great obligation, as it so nearly concerns the welfare of my friends in Boston. I have many things which I wish to say to Your Excellency, and most sincerely wish that I had broken through the formalities which I thought due to your rank and freely told you all I knew or thought of public affairs; and I must ever confess, whatever may be the event, that you generously gave me such opening, as I now think I ought to have embraced: but the true cause of my not doing it was the vileness and treachery of many persons around you, who, I suppose, had gained your entire confidence.

I am, &c.,

Joseph Warren"

The Exchange of Non-Combatants Leads to De Facto Recognition

General Thomas Gage indirectly replied to Dr. Joseph Warren's appeal when he participated in a two-day forum at Faneuil Hall.

On Saturday April 22, 1775, and continuing throughout the next day; British Military Governor General Thomas Gage and the Selectmen of Boston produced an agreement or understanding regarding the safe passage of civilians. This agreement was subsequently sent to Dr. Joseph Warren, President of the Massachusetts Provincial Congress and members of the Massachusetts Committee of Safety for approval. The nascent American-government of Massachusetts approved of this agreement or understanding. Civilians could now pass through the respective military lines without any repercussions. Sanity finally prevailed with everybody.

This agreement stated: "Gentlemen,- The Committee of Safety being informed that General Gage has proposed a treaty with the inhabitants of the town of Boston, whereby he stipulates that the women and children, with all their effects, shall have safe conduct without the garrison, and their men also, upon condition that the male inhabitants within the town, on their part, solemnly engage that they will not take up arms against the king's troops within the town, should an attack be made from without,- we cannot but esteem those conditions to be just and reasonable; and as the inhabitants are in danger of suffering from want of provisions, which, in this time of general confusion, cannot be conveyed into the town, we are willing you shall enter into and faithfully keep the engagement aforementioned, said to be required of you, and to remove yourselves, and your women, children, and effects, as soon as may be." (11)

General Thomas Gage requested a letter be sent to Dr. Joseph Warren. It said:

"That those persons in the country[side] who might incline to remove into Boston with their effects, might have liberty to do so without molestation." (12)

At Faneuil Hall, this agreement was approved unanimously by the Boston Selectmen and Military Governor General Thomas Gage.

On April 24, 1775, John Andrews wrote the following:

"Yesterday, we had town meetings all day, and finally concluded to deliver up all our arms to the Selectmen, on condition that the Governor would open the avenues to the town. In this agreement the townspeople were advised by the Committee of Safety to join. It requested that: the inhabitants deposit their arms promptly with the Selectmen. Accordingly, there were delivered to the Selectmen, and lodged in Faneuil Hall, 1,778 firearms, 634 pistols, 973 bayonets and 38 blunderbusses."

With one easy agreement, the otherwise incompetent General Gage was able to disarm the patriot civilians inside Boston and rid himself of potential armed-combatants. It was a deft and savvy maneuver by General Gage. As soon as the patriot civilians had relinquished their arms and delivered them to the Selectmen at Faneuil Hall, hundreds of people were then qualified to apply for the needed passes to leave the town. By May 6, 1775, half of the town's population had left Boston. Even Vice Admiral Graves agreed to lend small boats to help facilitate those wanting to leave.

Dr. Joseph Warren's adjuration was successful. General Gage was unburdened by the patriots of Boston and now they could leave. Loyalists could freely enter Boston to their welcomed relief.

The Free Independent Government and People of Massachusetts

The agreement or understanding between the British Military Governor General Thomas Gage and Dr. Joseph Warren, who was representing both the Congress of Massachusetts and the Massachusetts Committee of Safety, ergo became the first legal negotiations that had ever taken place between a representative of King George's government and the independent and legal civilian-government of the new State of Massachusetts. This simple act of negotiating, by the British government, vis-à-vis the legally created American government, by the free people of Massachusetts on April 23, 1775, was in fact a de facto recognition of Massachusetts as an independent state recognized by the British government. As a result, the people of Massachusetts became recognized as the first free and independent citizens of any American state. The citizens of Massachusetts simply acted on their inherent right to declare themselves to be free and independent, while rejecting their status as British subjects and discarding British rule. The British couldn't do anything about this reality except to offer warlike violence toward the Americans to keep them under British rule.

On April 23, 1775, after these negotiations were approved, the British remained exactly what they were to the people of Massachusetts, a foreign army of invaders occupying the territory of one Massachusetts town. The British military possessed no legal right to govern or occupy Boston, or be within the borders of any part of Massachusetts. The fledgling American nation, supported by most New Englanders, would do something about this state of affairs and soon.

For nearly two months, there were sporadic confrontations with small arms occasioned at the Boston Neck and the western, watery siege-lines. Shots were fired and reciprocated. Then all the fuss would become abated. The status quo stalemate between the Redcoats and the people of Massachusetts largely prevailed.

Prisoner Exchange

On June 6, 1775, an exchange of prisoners took place at the ferry dock in Charlestown. Wounded American prisoners captured by the British on April 19, 1775, and British prisoners captured that same day made their way back to their respective lines. Dr. Joseph Warren and General Israel Putnam represented the Americans and Major James Moncrief represented his king. Putnam and Moncrief were old friends and their working encounter was truly cordial. After an hour or two of pleasantries and some refreshments at Dr. Isaac Foster's house, the business of the exchange ended. Putnam, Warren and the Americans returned to Cambridge and Moncrief returned back to *HMS Lively*.

Too Little and Too Late With Insults and Name Calling

Having been infuriated for months, General Thomas Gage felt his courage rising with the arrival of reinforcements and the triumvirate of generals. The generals carried orders from London to instruct General Gage to declare Massachusetts to be in a state of rebellion and under martial law. The stage was being set by King George III and Prime Minister Lord North to proceed and put down the rebellion by armed force and have the war they wanted.

General Gage ordered the occasional literary playwright, General Gentleman Johnny Burgoyne to pen a proclamation on behalf of the British.

This proclamation was full of braggadocio and insults. General Burgoyne wrote the following:

"Whereas the infatuated multitudes, who have long suffered themselves to be conducted by certain well-known incendiaries and traitors, in a fatal progression of crimes against the constitutional authority of the state, have at length proceeded to avowed rebellion, and the good effects which were expected to arise from the patience and lenity of the king's government have been often frustrated, and are now rendered hopeless. By the influence of the same evil councils, it only remains for those who are intrusted with supreme rule, as well for the punishment of the guilty as the protection of the well-affected, to prove that they do not bear the sword in vain."

General Gage explained further, when he declared martial law:

"Those in arms and their abettors to be rebels and traitors." (13)

General Gage was willing to pardon any patriot who took up arms against King George III except two men, Samuel Adams and John Hancock. No reprieve would be offered for these two insurrectionists.

"The offences are of too flagitious a nature to admit of any other consideration than that of condign punishment." (14)

It's curious why American leaders such as: Dr. Joseph Warren, General Artemus Ward, Colonel William Prescott, General Israel Putnam and several other patriot leaders didn't make General Gage's most wanted list. All of these patriots were more than worthy to be held accountable as traitors for fomenting rebellion against the British.

Naturally the Tories were elated with this fustian declaration. They hoped that something positive might come from this proclamation. In contrast to loyalist beliefs, American patriots were deeply angered. This was clearly exhibited by Abigail Adams in her letter to her husband John Adams. John Adams was in Philadelphia, Pennsylvania attending the Second Continental Congress when he read her words. Abigail Adams wrote,

"Gage's Proclamation you will receive by this conveyance. All the records of time cannot produce a blacker page. Satan, when driven from the regions of bliss, exhibited not more malice. Surely the father of lies is superseded. Yet we think it the best proclamation he could have issued." (15)

Dr. Joseph Warren highly disliked General Gage's unremitting insults that he hurled toward the patriots and his condescending comments regarding the courage of the American militiamen. Dr. Warren confided in one of his pupils, William Eustis when he told him,

"They say we will not fight, and by God I hope I die up to my knees in British blood."

Not to be outdone by the British; the American leadership reciprocated General Gage by preparing their own counter proclamation. It offered amnesty to all the British, except, General Thomas Gage, Vice Admiral Samuel Graves, all the councilors who had not resigned from the Mandamus Council, Attorney General Johnathan Sewall, the two Commissioners of Customs, Charles Paxton and Benjamin Hallowell and all the Americans who went out with the British on April 19, 1775. Meaningful as the American counter proclamation was to the American patriots, it was never issued in public and just quietly faded away. The fast-moving events overshadowed it.

Nothing positive transpired from General Gage's incendiary words. Unknown to General Gage and his Redcoats; there were only five more days before a day of reckoning would be upon them. American retribution would be fired upon pompous General Thomas Gage and his occupying army of Redcoats. The fog of war was certain to be involved.

Part Two: The Battle of Bunker Hill

High-Ranking Traitor

A traitor lurked in the midst of the American leadership. This traitor was Dr. Benjamin Church. Thankfully for the American war effort, Dr. Church was not at the Committee of Safety meeting in Cambridge, but in Philadelphia on June 15, 1775. Church was sent to Philadelphia to deliver important correspondence to the Second Continental Congress.

Dr. Church was the chairman of the Committee of Safety and was clandestinely funneling American plans and intentions to General Gage for quite some time. Shrewd Dr. Joseph Warren suspected Dr. Church was a spy and traitor. At a Committee of Safety meeting, only two days after April 19, 1775, Dr. Church reportedly rose up from his chair to volunteer to ride into Boston and talk to General Gage. Dr. Joseph Warren was aghast at Dr. Church's proposal.

Dr. Warren asked him,

"Are you serious, Dr. Church? They will hang you if they catch you in Boston." Dr. Church was determined to go to Boston. Dr. Church was addiment. Again, he asked permission to go into Boston. Dr. Warren finally acquiesced and suggested to Church that he return with some medicine. A day and one-half passed by and Dr. Church successfully returned with the medicine. Dr. Church told tales about being arrested and interrogated by none other than General Gage himself.

Silversmith and patriot dispatch-rider Paul Revere was also suspicious of Dr. Church. Revere was informed by his network of patriot spies inside Boston, that Dr. Church and General Gage were seen in public conversing "like persons who had been long acquainted."

It was apparent that General Gage had little or no coherent acumen regarding his spying operations. Why would General Gage meet with Dr. Church so openly? It's quite amazing why it didn't occur to General Gage that to be seen in public with Dr. Church, a well-known and high-ranking rebel, would be potentially ruinous to his spying operations. General Thomas Gage's incompetence obviously had no boundaries.

If Dr. Benjamin Church had been in Cambridge on June 15, 1775, there is little doubt that he would have informed General Gage of the American plans. The American plans were only kept secret and secure because of the coincidence of the absence of Dr. Church.

Dr. Benjamin Church eventually was caught spying for the British. A written message by Dr. Church, which was entrusted to a woman to deliver to General Gage, was confiscated by patriots. The woman identified Dr. Church as the culprit who gave her the note for delivery. He was arrested and tried for treason. Dr. Church was then banished from Massachusetts and sent into exile. He was ordered to board a ship bound for the Caribbean. Dr. Church sailed away and was never seen again. Most likely he perished when the ship purportedly sank.

Let All of the Commotion Begin

In Cambridge a lot of commotion reigned inside the American camp. On June 16, 1775, General Ward and the Council of War decided to act upon the recommendations of the Committee of Safety. Officers present were: Commanding General Artemus Ward, Major General Dr. Joseph Warren, General Israel Putnam, General William Heath, Colonels William Prescott, Richard Gridley, Thomas Gardner, Henry Knox and Major John Brooks and some regimental commanders. Major General John Thomas and General Nathanael Greene were absent because they were commanding 5,000 men stationed at the Boston Neck. The old war-veteran General Seth Pomeroy was absent. He had returned home to Northampton a little more than 100 miles away. General Pomeroy left Cambridge before the Committee of Safety meeting the previous day. A messenger was dispatched to bring him back. General Pomeroy returned in time for the grand battle.

General Artemus Ward had no other choice but to fortify the heights of Charlestown. It became clear to General Ward and Dr. Joseph Warren that they were virtual sitting-ducks. The Americans couldn't wait for the British to arrive in Cambridge and scatter the troops. The American leadership was forced to act. Even though the British were seemingly bottled up in Boston; the Redcoats could have broken out by crossing over the Charles River to Cambridge or perhaps force their way out at the Boston Neck and then march directly to Cambridge. It would have been a fairly costly excursion for the British, but the most powerful army on the planet most likely could have achieved this objective.

General Ward's command was now severely tested. His ongoing concern of fretting about gunpowder wouldn't do him any good now. He simply had no other choice but to dole out the gunpowder and supply his troops. Most of the American gunpowder made its way to Charlestown, but General Ward still needed to keep some reserve gunpowder and account for it wisely. General Ward needed to protect Cambridge and the American leadership. Tragically, for the Americans, the lack of gunpowder would become a major shortfall at the Battle of Bunker Hill.

Acute awareness suddenly unfolded among the American militiamen. Gossip started to spread. The men became cognizant that a confrontation with the Redcoats was imminent. They were correct. The previous day they watched their officers scurry back and forth. They were going in and out of General Ward's headquarters. Electrifying news would soon be officially passed on to the men. General Artemus Ward and the Council of War had decided to act. The men would be on their way to occupy Charlestown that night! The men knew that this action would surely draw the British out for a fight. They prepared themselves as best that they could. They were waiting for this eventuality for nearly two months.

It had only been a few days since General Thomas Gage had released his bombastic diatribe upon the American nation. American patriots would have their own statement to make starting the night of June 16, 1775.

General Artemus Ward and the recently promoted Major General Dr. Joseph Warren, along with members of the Committee of Safety, had known about General Gage's breakout plan for a couple of days and had made counter plans. The time had come for American valor to make a stand. Perhaps some luck would favor the side of the American patriots. They were preparing to check the advances of General Gage and his Redcoats. They would need all the luck that they could muster.

The Road Leads to Charlestown

Camp dust rose up from the hooves of scampering horses. All the American regiments were assembling on the Cambridge Common. The call-to-arms had finally come. For some men, like Colonel William Prescott and General Israel Putnam, the call-to-arms didn't come fast enough. The time for action had finally arrived. The American leaders were ready!

It was early in the evening around six o'clock when company sergeants barked out their orders to the men. Some of the Americans were still struggling and unfamiliar with military protocol. They scrambled into position. They were informed by their elected officers that they would be marching to the Charlestown Peninsula that evening. Most of the militiamen didn't know where the Charlestown Peninsula was. Once in Charlestown, they would be building some sort of fortification. Wagons were then summoned by Captain Foster to load the entrenching tools. Shovels and spades, pickaxes, pitchforks and any type of earth-breaking tool, plus some carpentry tools, were loaded onto the wagons for the short trip to Charlestown. The men were ordered to bring blankets and provisions for one day. The reality of this command, to only bring supplies for one day, would become quite dangerous for the erelong toiling-men. Most of the patriots ignored this order at their peril. The fog of war now fully embedded with the Americans held close to the troops.

On the Cambridge Common, there were some volunteer-militiamen who saw action on the battle road from Lexington and Concord on April 19, 1775. But most of the Americans never fired a weapon in anger and were military novices. To their benefit, they were led by a handful of old and trusted seasoned-veterans. Virtually all of the high-ranking American-veterans had served with the British in the French and Indian War. The young patriots were facing the challenge of a lifetime. They were encouraged to make a last will and testament. The military reality of the American Revolution was now front and center and its character was very harrowing for everybody.

The local men mustering on the Cambridge Common, who hailed from Charlestown, had already lost their homes to the British. Their families were scattered throughout the Massachusetts countryside. The Townies were seeking revenge against these foreign invaders who drove away their families. In less than twenty-four-hours, even more disaster would befall the Townies. But the patriot men from Charlestown had friends, approximately 10,310 friends. Their new friends came from every area of New England. They were lining up with the Townies to punish and push the British out of Boston and Massachusetts. The Townies of Charlestown would eventually have their chance to fight. They impatiently waited for their opportunity.

At about seven o'clock, after receiving their orders to march to Charlestown; the militiamen gathered together on the Cambridge Common to listen to an impassioned prayer and to receive their blessings. The orator was the President of Harvard College, Rev. Samuel Langdon. Langdon was born in Boston and was an ardent patriot. Langdon was an ordained minister and a classmate of Samuel Adams. He climbed on top of a small stage and started to address the men. Perhaps at this precise moment; Langdon's prayers, blessings and encouraging words helped subdue the anxiety inflicting the American patriots. The day long

commotion in their camp had provided lots of apprehension and disquie-
tude. These amateur American-soldiers were understandably anxious of
the imminent future. They were pondering their personal fate.

After the sun had set on this late spring day, the sky would reveal a
clear moonlit night. All written accounts confirm that at nine o'clock, at
least 1,200 American militiamen started to make their way to the
Charlestown Peninsula. (16) Leading the way was Colonel William Prescott. He was wearing his long blue-coat, a tri-cornered hat and carrying
his sword. Two sergeants were marching in front of him with darkened
lanterns. Colonel William Prescott's Regiment, Colonel Ebenezer
Bridge's Regiment and Colonel James Frye's Regiment, led by his second
in command, Lt. Colonel Dr. James Brickett, all marched toward the
Charlestown Neck. Colonel Frye was incapacitated. He was suffering
from gout. Captain Samuel Gridley, son of Engineer Colonel Richard
Gridley and his 49 men, followed closely behind lugging two artillery-
guns. And behind them all were several wagons full of the entrenching
tools in the care of Captain Foster. The men marched briskly but quietly.
Their footsteps echoed the sounds of freedom. It was roughly a three-mile
trek to the heights of Charlestown.

Arriving at the Charlestown Peninsula

Near the Charlestown Neck, Massachusetts militiamen were joined by
General Israel Putnam and his 300 men from Connecticut. The Connecticut militiamen were also led by Captain Thomas Knowlton. Twenty-three-
year-old Major John Brooks from Colonel Bridge's Regiment had also
arrived at the neck and joined his regiment. (Major John Brooks became
Governor of Massachusetts in 1816 and was the first President of the Bunker Hill Monument Association). The Americans proceeded to cross over
the Charlestown Neck and were ordered to stop and wait at the base of
Bunker Hill. The Americans then proceeded to the crest of Bunker Hill
and were ordered to stop once more. Colonel Prescott then ordered a company of his own men, led by Captain John Nutting and ten men from the
Connecticut ranks, to scout along the shore road to find suitable positions
in the village of Charlestown to support their mission.

Meanwhile American troops waited for more orders. Again, they proceeded. They continued to march to the south side of Bunker Hill and
stopped once more. It was here that Colonel William Prescott, General
Israel Putnam, Engineer Colonel Richard Gridley and another reportedly

unknown general took part in a heated debate. Who was this supposed second general? Nobody knows. His name is apparently lost forever. Not one of the following generals was present at this discussion; General Artemus Ward was in Cambridge, Major General Dr. Joseph Warren was also in Cambridge, or perhaps nearby in Watertown, General William Heath was in Cambridge, Major General John Thomas and General Nathanael Greene were in Roxbury at the Boston Neck and General Seth Pomeroy was returning from Northampton. Perhaps we will never know who this fourth officer was unless some documentation is finally discovered. And perhaps, just maybe, Major John Brooks was the fourth officer and was mistaken for a general.

The orders issued on June 15, 1775, explicitly stated to fortify the 110-foot Bunker Hill. The American officers talked, debated and argued their opinions and ideas of where to build the redoubt. Would the American officers follow their orders? Or would the Americans fortify the smaller sixty-five-foot unnamed hill? Did they consider the smaller appendix part of Bunker Hill or not? It's likely that the officers were trying to decipher their exact orders. None of the officers were from Charlestown and maybe to the American leadership, the prominent heights on the Charlestown Peninsula all constituted Bunker Hill. A decision had to be made soon.

It must have been obvious to the militiamen that their officers were struggling to decide exactly where to build the redoubt. Eventually Engineer Colonel Richard Gridley reminded everyone that time was critical; now was the time to start fortifying some area and do it promptly. Amazingly it took nearly two hours to decide where to build the redoubt. Why did it take nearly two hours for the officers to come to a final conclusion and continue on to Russell's Pasture? We will never know why. Onward to the smaller hill the American troops marched accompanied by the fog of war.

It was now well past 11 o'clock and quickly approaching midnight. Colonel Prescott and his troops proceeded to march down the gradual southern-slope of Bunker Hill toward the smaller hill. The Americans finally stopped marching and settled upon Russell's Pasture. As explained earlier, Russell's Pasture was situated on this smaller hill, or appendage to Bunker Hill. This smaller hill eventually became known as Breed's Hill. This is where the redoubt was built.

Sometime after the heated discussion on Bunker Hill was over, General Putnam rode back to Cambridge. In Cambridge he reported to General

Ward regarding the decision to build a redoubt on Breed's Hill. General Putnam then attempted to get a few moments of rest, as he was planning to make his way back to Charlestown in short time.

On to Russell's Pasture

Arriving at Russell's Pasture, situated upon the smaller hill, Colonel Richard Gridley started to measure out the dimensions of the little fort. When Colonel Gridley finished, the Americans started to dig and construct their redoubt. The men were instructed to be as quiet as possible. That would be difficult considering the task at hand. After a couple of hours of digging, Colonel Prescott told his men not to be so concerned with some noise. The redoubt had to be finished quickly as possible.

The decision to build the redoubt on Breed's Hill proved to be a major tactical error. As mentioned earlier, Bunker Hill rose 110-feet above Boston Harbor and the steep, southern-slope was almost impregnable. Being further from Boston Harbor, Bunker Hill would have been out of range from the cannons on British warships and also from Copp's Hill. The 65-foot Breed's Hill was virtually untenable. It had gently rising-slopes on all sides and would be within easy range of cannons once the British hauled them over to Charlestown. General Putnam had argued the Americans should first fortify Bunker Hill. This fort would cover the American retreat if necessary. Otherwise, if the Americans were defeated, they would have to cross the narrow Charlestown Neck, while the British fired at them from above. If the Americans fortified both hills, they could safely retire to Bunker Hill or retreat off the peninsula entirely without much concern of being trapped or routed. As the historical facts reveal, the sole redoubt was built on Breed's Hill and not Bunker Hill. After the Battle of Bunker Hill, the Committee of Safety said that the selection of Breed's Hill was a mistake. (17) Amidst all the American confusion, there can be no doubt that the fog of war had helped lead the Americans to Breed's Hill.

Entrenching Tools Expedite the Small Earthen-Redoubt

In Boston and on the royal warships, sentries proclaimed all is well. Yet, it wasn't all that well for the British and they would soon find out why. The only British officer who believed the Americans were up to something clandestine, was General Henry Clinton. General Clinton claimed in his memoirs that he had reconnoitered the village of Charlestown on the night of June 16, 1775. He writes that he had either seen or heard the Americans at work. He doesn't say where he was or what he may have thought the Americans were doing. In addition, incompetent British sentries reportedly had heard the rebels at work all night-long without reporting it. In the morning the sentries mentioned this activity only in casual conversations.

General Clinton immediately reported the rebel activity to General Gage and to General Howe. General Clinton strongly suggested that at the break of dawn, British troops should at once be landed in Charlestown. General Howe also wanted British troops to move posthaste. General Gage snubbed the warnings and said he didn't think much of the American activities. General Gage said he wanted to wait until the morning so he could observe the intentions of the Americans. Once again, General Gage displayed a lack of enthusiasm to pursue the enemy. This decision spoke volumes regarding his lack of competency to lead an army.

Concerned that his troops would soon be discovered, Colonel Prescott made two trips, along with Major John Brooks, to reconnoiter the banks of the Charles River. Colonel Prescott heard for himself the sentry call of all is well. This must have assuaged Colonel Prescott to some extent.

Colonel Prescott's men had been laboring and working very hard during the early morning hours of June 17, 1775. The men worked in shifts. One hour of digging was relieved by one hour of standing watch. By 3:30 a.m., the Americans were tired, hungry and thirsty. The men's current discomfort was just a small prelude to the anguish they would experience in the coming daylight-hours. The American militiamen were about to fight the best trained army in the world, but the odds of victory were stacked against them. To win this battle and to help secure their liberties, the American militiamen would have to be very disciplined and follow exactly all the orders coming from their veteran officers. Would they be capable to engage with the Redcoats? Understandably, the Americans were scared.

Incredibly in just four hours, from midnight till 4 a.m., the main structure of the redoubt had materialized. Since most of the American men were farmers, they knew precisely how to maximize their entrenching tools. The earthen redoubt was taking its grand form. Colonel Richard Gridley's measurements were approximately 8 rods (132-feet) square and the redoubt walls were roughly six-feet-high. There was a small redan (triangular shaped walls) facing Charlestown to the southeast. The Americans also built a ditch in front and to the sides of the fort. There was also a firing platform inside the redoubt. It was built to support the four cannons from where Captain Samuel Gridley and Captain John Callender presumably would be firing at the British. In their haste to finish the redoubt, the patriots forgot to create a few embrasures in the redoubt walls for their cannons to fire through. In a somewhat jocular escapade, the Americans were eventually compelled to blast out their embrasures by firing their way through the redoubt's walls. The fog of war had now entered the American redoubt.

There were two entrances or exit openings to the redoubt; one was toward the back looking out to the southwest and one looked to the northwest toward the rail fence and the Mystic River. Although this small redoubt was built in the darkness and roughly in only six-hours, it would provide the shelter that the Americans would need on top of Breed's Hill.

Early Morning Cannons Awaken Boston

Shortly after 4 a.m. the first hint of daylight had appeared. The natural fog was now slowly dissipating. There was an inkling of a clear beautiful-New England day on the horizon following a clear starlit-night. And the baleful fog of war was preparing to make many appearances on this day.

A sentry on board *HMS Lively* moored only a short distance from the redoubt, looked out in amazement toward the heights of Charlestown. He saw what was on top of the Charlestown Heights. He hurried to inform the ship's clerk about this amazing structure on top of Breed's Hill. It was an American fort! It had appeared overnight!

Once informed of the redoubt, Captain Thomas Bishop who recently received a court-martial for negligence, quickly turned his ship around by placing a spring on the cable. His broadside faced the redoubt and he fired his cannons. Bang! Suddenly a thunderous noise rang out. This tremendous rumble rattled window panes and everything inside Boston. General Thomas Gage along with all of his Redcoats and everybody else in the town of Boston, were suddenly awakened from their slumber to the sounds of cannonballs roaring out of British cannons. This thunderous noise permeated the morning silence again and again.

After the first few British shots were fired, a row boat was observed leaving the warship and quickly heading over to Boston. Its occupants were making their way to the British high command. Shortly afterwards, Vice Admiral Graves ordered the bombardment from *HMS Lively* to stop. This respite didn't last long. Vice Admiral Graves then signaled to *HMS Lively* once again and this time it was to renew the firing. Within one minute the cannon blasts recommenced. Despite General Gage's negligence pertaining to the unknown early-morning-activities by the Americans, certainly now there could be no mistake where they were. General Thomas Gage now understood exactly where the American position was. They were on top of Breed's Hill overlooking Boston! The American patriots were boldly proclaiming to General Gage; here we are come get us!

On the small fortified hilltop, brave but inexperienced American warriors were about to face elite British-soldiers from the world's strongest empire. Dreadfully, the Royal Navy had already started to cannonade them. The Americans briefly stopped working after the first British shots were fired. It was simultaneously a magnificent and terrorizing sight to behold. The young American-farmers dropped their tools and ran to the walls of the redoubt to gaze at *HMS Lively*. The cannon blasts had mesmerized them. Their little fort had been discovered and now they were targets of the British. Feelings of trepidation and anguish engulfed the men. Colonel Prescott commanded them to finish the job of building their nascent little-fort. They complied with his orders and tried to shore up the redoubt as best that they could. Colonel Prescott also implored his men to stay within the redoubt and not to venture outside of it. They grew more frightened by the minute.

The sunrise had revealed a critical tactical-error by the Americans. Colonel Prescott looked out and realized that to the immediate north and south of the redoubt, the terrain was wide open, courtesy of the fog of war. Colonel Prescott then ordered a breastwork, 165-feet long to be constructed on the north side of the hill. It ended at a swampy area. This swampy area was near the narrow beach of the Mystic River. Colonel Prescott did this in his attempt to protect the left flank of the redoubt. To the south, nothing practical could be done to protect the redoubt. The village of Charlestown lay at the foot of Breed's Hill and this was going to have to be good enough for any covering action to the south. There was only time to send out one work detail and that would be to the north side of the hill. The men grabbed their pickaxes, spades and shovels. They went to work. Quickly the Americans started to break the hillside ground and started to build the breastwork. This hurriedly built breastwork to the north of the little redoubt was the only practical area to build any kind of worthwhile flanking-fortification. British cannonading once again commenced.

By 8 o'clock, a steady stream of cannonballs continued to be fired at the American positions. Luckily for the Americans, British cannons couldn't reach the redoubt because of the angle that the cannons had to be fired. The cannons were compromised by the height and distance of the hill. The British did manage to destroy two hogsheads that held a sizable amount of water. The loss of the hogsheads was critical.

All throughout the morning and during the raging battle, raking cannon fire came from the Copp's Hill battery, the warships *HMS Lively, HMS Falcon, HMS Glasgow, HMS Symmetry* and several floating gondolas.

It was around this time in the morning that the first American-casualty had occurred. A party of men, who had left their work detail at the breastwork, were making their way to Charlestown. They were leaving to obtain some water. This is when a cannonball fired from a warship hit and decapitated Asa Pollard of Billerica. The men who were with Pollard were stunned. Some of Pollard's remains were splattered upon them. None of these men had ever seen anything resembling this spine-chilling horror. Other men dropped their shovels and came running over from the breastwork. They too were aghast by the sight of Pollard's lifeless body. Apparently, some of the men felt the need to witness this ghastly calamity. The patriots wanted to bury their friend Asa Pollard. They wanted to include a small religious-service for him. In short time Colonel Prescot had arrived and asked who the man was. One man then asked Colonel Prescott, "What should we do?" They wanted to know if they could bury Pollard with a small religious-ceremony. A two-word answer is all that came from Colonel Prescott. He said, "Bury him." Again, the men were stunned. But this time they were stunned from the stern and stringent comment made by their colonel. How could they bury Pollard without a moment of prayer and reflection? Colonel Prescott remained firm and ordered his men back to work building the breastwork. Colonel Prescott may have appeared callous, but he was pragmatic. Colonel Prescott didn't want his men to have the time to agonize over Pollard's death and scare themselves even more than they already were. There was work to be done. The safety of everybody was at stake. Colonel Prescott knew that the wellbeing of his men was dependent upon him doling out discipline. Without asking any more questions the men buried Asa Pollard.

The British Plan of the Day

General Thomas Gage hastily called his war council together at Province House. The officers present were: Major General William Howe, Major General Henry Clinton, Major General Johnny Burgoyne, General Hugh Percy, General Valentine Jones, Lt. Colonel Robert Pigot, who was temporarily promoted to the rank of brevetted brigadier general, Lt. Colonel James Abercromby, Major John Pitcairn and Vice Admiral Samuel Graves who represented the Royal Navy and several other adjutant officers and aides-de-camp.

Loyalist militia leader General Timothy Ruggles was allowed to attend the morning meeting. Ruggles had organized the Loyal Association of Massachusetts and managed to recruit only a partial regiment of men. Ruggles and his loyalist militia were never even close to being a military factor in the struggle for Massachusetts. Loyalist Ruggles appreciated and understood the character of his enemies. He knew that the patriots would fight the Redcoats to their death if need be. After exiting the Province House meeting, Ruggles said to a fellow loyalist,

"It would cost many lives to attack in front; but the English officers would not believe that the Americans would fight."

Ruggles advised that the British attack should be made as a rearguard maneuver. This would cut off any retreat and prevent reinforcements from entering the battle. (18)

Loyalist Timothy Ruggles' words rang-out loud and they rang-out clear. But Ruggles' concept only mattered to those who understood the American warriors. That wasn't anybody in the British high-command, especially General Thomas Gage and General William Howe. American Timothy Ruggles was ignored.

Woe is Henry

When the Province House meeting commenced, General Henry Clinton immediately started speaking about the proposed strategy that he had suggested only a few hours earlier.

The length of the Charlestown Peninsula, from the Charlestown Neck to Boston Harbor, was just a little over one-mile long. It had a shape similar to that of a pear. General Clinton proposed to land troops in Charlestown near the ferry dock. In conjunction with this troop landing; he wanted to land troops to the rear of the Americans at the Charlestown Neck. With the help of the Royal Navy, troops would simply travel down the Mystic River to the northern-coast of the peninsula. They would merely float by American positions on the hills. Once at the neck and behind the rebels, the Redcoats would block the only escape route which the rebels had. The British would simply bottle-up the Americans and the day would be won. It would be easy.

General Gage and his subordinate generals, along with the other high-ranking officers, didn't like General Clinton's plan. But the always prepared General Clinton had a secondary plan. He suggested that all of the British troops could land near the village of Charlestown, or near the cemetery, on the south side of the peninsula. They would then be split in two and some of the Redcoats would march along the south side of the peninsula to the Charlestown Neck. General Clinton proposed that this action would produce the same result. General Clinton said that the Royal Navy should also bombard and rake the Charlestown Neck, while anchored near the area of the Mill Pond. This would prevent any Americans from entering or leaving Charlestown. General Clinton's plan was simple and straightforward. Most likely, General Clinton's plan would have worked.

Much of General Clinton's plan made military sense. As General Clinton had previously suggested to General Gage and General Howe, General Clinton wanted to deploy troops immediately. Yet both General Gage and General Howe immediately rejected General Clinton's overall plan or any plan that he would have presented.

General Gage continued on with his seemingly endless procrastination. That was easy for him to do since he thought that the Americans wouldn't stand up to his Redcoats. He mistakenly believed they would run like rabbits.

For officers like General Gage and General Howe their personal and stubborn pride mirrored the haughty pride of the entire British Empire. Perhaps both General Gage and General Howe may have thought that some of General Clinton's plan might be solid, but they would never admit to this. This is something that we will never know.

General Burgoyne kept mostly silent. He didn't have much input other than to side with General Gage and General Howe. It was easy for General Burgoyne to side with General Gage and General Howe. General Burgoyne had nothing but contempt for the Americans. As far as General Burgoyne was concerned, the Redcoats would push the rebels off the hilltop very quickly utilizing their planned assault. General John Burgoyne would have an easy-chair job during the attack. He would be on Copp's Hill in Boston helping to direct that battery.

The clock was ticking off time. General Gage continued to dawdle throughout the morning. He wasn't in a rush. Yet every minute that British troops were not engaged on the battlefield, the stronger the rebels became.

Lamentably for General Henry Clinton, his peers projected an air of piddling toward his military plans. He was not held in high esteem by his fellow officers. Perhaps one of the reasons Clinton's plan was rejected, was simply his insufferable personality. General Clinton was an annoying man. He was quick to detect any type of small slight directed toward him, regardless whether it was real or imagined. Then Clinton would brood over it. Additionally, General Clinton came from the "German-School" of British military-experience. This meant that he learned his trade on the continent of Europe and not somewhere in the backwater of North America. General Clinton attempted to project an impression of superiority. His personality was compounded by the fact that he was a loner. These were not good traits to have as a British major general.

The British generals at the Province House meeting didn't want to play second fiddle to a man to whom they simply didn't like. If any accolades were going to be doled out after the battle, it would be on their behalf and not bestowed upon General Henry Clinton. It didn't matter what plan General Henry Clinton proposed. It would never be good enough for the others in that room. At every opportunity they dismissed General Clinton's plan. Regardless, General Gage and General Howe already decided the type of assault which they would implement. The British would march up the hill and into the redoubt. The fog of war easily led the British generals to their decision.

Both General Gage and General Howe were adamant against landing troops at the Charlestown Neck. They argued this would be too risky because of the unknown strength and troop placement of the Americans. This was a valid concern. General Gage opined that an amphibious landing was problematic. The British didn't have any flat-bottom boats to navigate the shallow water along the mud flats. Astoundingly, Vice Admiral Graves had never sounded the Mystic River or placed a warship there. Also, marching troops to the neck presented the same problems once they arrived. Perhaps the British would be caught between two American forces, one already on the peninsula and another coming from the mainland. Again, this was a valid concern. If the Americans would not come out to fight as predicted, then the whole debate about landing troops at the neck was a moot point.

General Gage and General Howe simply brushed aside General Clinton's strategy to land troops far to the rear of the Americans at the Charlestown Neck. They would have none of it. For this fateful decision and more tragically for the British soldiers, it would be General Thomas Gage's men who would ultimately pay a costly price. The fog of war would soon hand General Gage and General Howe the bill that was due. Misperceptions by General Gage and General Howe would essentially rue their day on June 17, 1775.

General Gage and General Howe fervently believed that they could parade their troops and easily march up Breed's Hill without much or any opposition. They surmised that the Americans would suddenly surrender at the sight of the grand British Army. This New England rabble would just run away. This collection of pompous British-generals believed that the American rebellion would begin to be dismantled that very day. From Charlestown, British troops would chase the panicked rebels away and then continue marching all the way to Cambridge. The British planned to capture the rebel leaders and crush the seeds of American liberty.

To the American left, the British planned to attack from the Mystic River beach and would feign a frontal attack on the redoubt. Once on the beach, the British assumed they would be hidden from view because of the beach bluffs. Attacking from the beach, the British would flank the American left. To the American right, the British would attack through Charlestown and charge up Breed's Hill into the redoubt. This was the uncomplicated British battle plan. It would be the only approved and scheduled plan. There was no need for a secondary plan.

General Howe's orders were specific. Once deployed, his troops would carry three days of provisions that included food and a full knapsack of supplies. General Howe intended to arrive at American headquarters in Cambridge by nightfall. Unlike the volunteer American-militiamen, who could simply leave at any time and without fear of any punishment; the conscripted British Redcoats had the wrath of death imposed upon anyone if he deserted. In General Howe's orders, he said,

"Any man who shall quit his rank on any pretense or shall dare to plunder or pillage will be executed without mercy."

One positive factor for the British emanating from the Province House meeting was; General William Howe was appointed the field commander.

He was indomitable and considered the best light infantry-general that the British could deploy to any battlefield. He was an excellent military-tactician. Prior to his assignment to Boston, General Howe was never defeated in battle. He would have ample opportunity to showcase his abilities in a mere few hours' time.

The collective mindset of the British Council of War believed the Americans scoundrels would not fight. This fallacious belief was all that the British needed to satisfy and assure themselves of an easy victory. Perhaps the British military-leadership developed amnesia. Perhaps they forgot about the day of April 19, 1775. Recently at the Battle of Lexington and Concord, the Americans gave the British lion a severe drubbing. One can only conjecture why General Thomas Gage and his top officers didn't remember this fact. The British had absolutely no respect for the American fighting-man.

The urgent meeting at Province House produced the only decision that would satisfy both General Thomas Gage and General William Howe. The breathtaking display of the British military-might would be unveiled for all to behold. This would be an easy battle for the Redcoats. A quick British victory would correct the political course of Massachusetts and bring it back into the British Empire's fold.

On the Charlestown Heights, the American rebels would simultaneously be participants and the audience of this grand spectacle. They were expected to run away from their front row center-seats. As far as the British were concerned, the Americans needed to be clobbered into submission. The British military would be released to destroy the rebels and they couldn't wait to do it. But what the British didn't know was; the fog of war was now firmly entrenched within its army.

On With It

It was mid-morning when the meeting at Province House was finished. Directly afterward, General Thomas Gage made one of his infrequent forays to the Boston shoreline to observe the battlefield. A loyalist by the name of Abijah Willard had accompanied General Gage. The British commander was looking through his spyglass and studying the American stronghold. General Gage observed Colonel Prescott walking back and forth on top of the redoubt walls. Colonel Prescott was encouraging his men to be ready and above all, to keep fueling the flames of courage inside themselves. While General Gage studied the rebel works, he handed

Willard the spyglass and asked if he could identify the tall commanding-figure on the parapet. Willard looked, he turned to Gage and said it was William Prescott his own brother-in-law.

"Will he fight?" Gage demanded.

"I cannot answer for his men," Willard replied, "but Prescott will fight you to the gates of hell."

By mid-morning, the Americans had been digging and building their redoubt and breastwork for nine hours. They still weren't finished with it. The men were fatigued, hungry and thirsty. The air temperature was rising quickly. It began to get very warm, especially inside the redoubt. Complaints were beginning to be heard. The patriots wanted to know when reinforcements and refreshments would arrive. Nobody had an answer for the men. Sadly, many Americans had disregarded their order to bring one day's worth of provisions for themselves. The personal-neglect of this direct order was becoming each American's personal-suffering. The patriots woeful neglect of this order had been approved by the fog of war.

While Waiting for the Enemy

Approximately around the time that General Gage was wrapping-up his Province House meeting, Colonel Prescott was having a Council of War on top of Breed's Hill. The American officers all agreed that their men were not in any state to fight a battle. Men were deserting their posts. Dozens and dozens of men just simply walked away. The grumblings of their condition continued. The American reality was; Colonel Prescott knew there wouldn't be initial reinforcements coming anytime soon. Some of the officers were unabated with their demands for fresh troops. Colonel Prescott became weary of this ongoing conversation. He bluntly conveyed to his officers that the men who had raised the redoubt walls were the best able to defend them. They had learned to despise the fire from the enemy. They deserved to have the honor of the victory. Colonel Prescott's men had earned his respect and in return, respect was given to him.

After listening to his officers and at their insistence; Colonel Prescott acceded to send Major John Brooks back to General Artemus Ward's headquarters to ask for food and drink and if possible and to send more troops. Major Brooks was ordered to find a horse for his trip. The only horses available were the artillery horses. Major Brooks asked Captain Samuel Gridley for a horse and Captain Gridley refused to give him one.

Captain Gridley said he needed the horses to pull the cannons to his post. Major Brooks proceeded to travel as fast as he could to Cambridge on foot.

Along the road, Major Brooks met General Putnam. General Putnam had been awakened by the thundering guns of *HMS Lively* and was returning to inspect the redoubt. The two men had a brief discussion about the immediate events and then parted.

It was now around 10 o'clock and Major Brooks had finally arrived at General Ward's headquarters. Shortly after Major Brooks had arrived, General Ward was being beseeched by Brooks to send reinforcements. The future governor pleaded with the commanding general, but General Ward was still reluctant to send men. He wanted to have as many men at the ready if the British broke through the American lines. General Ward's position was prudent military-strategy and he was determined to stay with this plan. He couldn't leave Cambridge defenseless at this critical hour.

General Ward then attended the Committee of Safety meeting in an adjacent room. General Ward was doing his best to remain primed for an attack on Cambridge. There were several questions to be discussed. What if General Gage was just feigning an attack on Charlestown and was planning instead to breakout of Boston at the Boston Neck? Major General John Thomas was at the Boston Neck, but would he be able to contain the British? What if General Gage's troops crossed the Charles River from the Back-Bay and landed in Cambridge? Or would there be a British landing closer to Lechmere's Point? If any of these scenarios happened, General Ward would need his reserve troops. Rightfully, General Artemus Ward needed to hold back enough troops to protect the civilians of Cambridge and the political leaders of Massachusetts. Although criticized for being too cautious, General Ward couldn't afford to deploy all of his troops to Charlestown, because this would-be folly. General Ward was also suffering from a bad case of bladder stone. His ailment almost incapacitated him. But like a good soldier, General Artemus Ward persevered throughout the day from his command post in Cambridge.

General Putnam was riding his steed as fast as the animal could go. As he approached and crossed over the Charlestown Neck, he was braving a British chainshot-barrage from *HMS Symmetry*. He was the first American to run this Royal Navy gauntlet. While in Cambridge, General William Heath had reminded General Putnam to gather up all the valuable entrenching tools. General Putnam finally arrived back at the redoubt. He looked surprised and disgusted that nobody had taken the initiative to begin building fortifications on Bunker Hill. General Putnam then asked Colonel Prescott for volunteers to gather all the entrenching tools and proceed back to Bunker Hill. Colonel Prescott initially was averse to General Putnam's request. Eventually Colonel Prescott finally agreed to General Putnam's plea. This action would ultimately become a costly mistake. The fog of war had just hit the Americans and it hit the Americans hard.

Hurriedly dozens of men grabbed a tool and started to proceed up to Bunker Hill. It was a rush to find a tool. The entrenching tools represented a free-pass out of the redoubt and further away from foreign soldiers who had orders to attack and kill Americans. All morning long, Colonel Prescott had been losing men to desertion and fatigue. He was extremely reluctant to lose anymore. Colonel Prescott believed that whoever went to Bunker Hill wouldn't make their way back to the redoubt. He was correct. Nobody returned. Many of these men stayed on top of Bunker Hill for the duration of the battle as useless malingering-witnesses.

Once again, General Putnam left the heights of Charlestown and rode back to Cambridge to attend the Committee of Safety meeting. At this meeting, both General Putnam and General Ward presented their divergent arguments about sending more troops to Charlestown. Most of the civilian members of the Committee of Safety sided with General Ward. But he was cautioned by them to have all of his regiments prepared to march to Charlestown or any other place at a moment's notice. It was also at this time that General Ward felt the need to remind General Putnam that it was he that was in charge and not General Putnam.

Before the meeting concluded, Major John Brooks spoke to the Committee of Safety. He implored the committee to send more troops to Charlestown. Although the Committee of Safety had just listened to General Ward and to General Putnam, the committee may have been swayed by the pleading of Major Brooks. Major Brooks was followed by a committee member and a resident of Charlestown. His name was Richard Devens. Devens delivered an impassioned speech in favor of sending reinforcements to Charlestown. The Committee of Safety proceeded to vote affirmatively to send reinforcements. Reluctantly General Ward agreed to the appeal.

Meanwhile Major General Dr. Joseph Warren was suffering from a severe headache and most likely running a fever. He was exhausted and laying in bed upstairs. He didn't attend the Committee of Safety meeting.

Dr. Warren had been up all-night attending to the business of the Massachusetts Provincial Congress in Watertown.

Major General Dr. Joseph Warren was wearing many hats during the last five turbulent-years. He was navigating his political positions skillfully while partaking in his medical-endeavors assiduously. He was constantly on the move, keeping late hours attempting to guide his countrymen toward freedom and liberty. On the precipice of a stupendous battle, the stresses which he must have felt had finally caught up to him.

After General Ward finally acquiesced to send more troops; he sent a dispatch rider to Medford and ordered Colonel John Stark of New Hampshire to march to Charlestown. Before Colonel Stark left Medford, his men had to make their own bullets. From Cambridge they had received some lead from a church organ which had been dismantled. They melted down the lead and remolded it into musketballs. They departed as soon as they could.

Upon their arrival at the Charlestown Neck; Colonel Stark's men were carrying a variety of old muskets and guns and a meager amount of ammunition with very little gunpowder. Eventually Colonel Stark's regiment met up with Colonel James Reed's regiment closely positioned near the Charlestown Neck. Colonel Reed was absent due to illness. Colonel Stark took command of Reed's regiment further augmenting his own force which made it the largest American regiment. Colonel Stark and the New Hampshire troops then braved the raking crossfire from the British floating-batteries. The gondolas were firing from either side of the neck without too much precision.

One of these New Hampshire men was Henry Dearborn. He was a young captain serving directly under Colonel Stark. Dearborn recalled that his company was out in front of the New Hampshire regiment and that he marched beside Colonel Stark. They were moving quickly as they crossed over the Charlestown Neck. The British were raking the neck with deadly crossfire when he suggested to Colonel Stark that they should quicken their pace. Colonel Stark calmly looked at Captain Dearborn and told him that, "one fresh man in action is worth ten fatigued ones."

Once over the neck, Colonel Stark marched his men to the top of Bunker Hill. There he talked to General Israel Putnam who was urging some men to build fortifications on this vital hilltop. Colonel Stark looked to the north and then to the south and assessed the military situation. He immediately knew where he was needed the most. Nobody had to tell this veteran warrior where to go. He quickly led his men down the slope of Bunker Hill to the rail fence. He would soon be on the Mystic River beach.

Serving in Colonel John Stark's regiment was Major Andrew McClary. McClary was a behemoth of a man standing six-foot six-inches-tall and was well liked by his fellow warriors. McClary was encouraging the men to be prepared. McClary had led a raid six months earlier on a castle in Portsmouth, New Hampshire where he was able to seize the muskets that many of the New Hampshire troops possessed.

Eventually some of the New Hampshire men went down to the Mystic River beach with Colonel Stark. They partially dismantled an existing stone wall that was on top of the bluffs. With these stones they built a small stone-wall on the beach for protection. This stone wall ran from the base of the nine-foot high-bluffs to the edge of the Mystic River. It was a small beach with a width of only twelve-feet. It was here that they waited for the British.

Scarlet Redcoats Everywhere

By mid-morning, General Gage issued orders for British Regiments to begin mustering for their deployment to Charlestown. They are as follows:

The ten oldest companies of Grenadiers, and the ten oldest companies of light infantry, the 5th and 38th Regiments to parade, half after eleven o'clock, with their Arms, Ammunitions, Blankets, and provisions ordered to be cooked this morning; they will march by files to the Long Warf.

The 52nd and 43rd Regiments, with the remaining companies of Grenadiers and light infantry, to parade at the same time, with the same direction, and march to the North Battery. The 47th and First Battalion of Royal Marines, will also march as above directed to the North Battery, after the rest are embarked, and be ready to embark when ordered. The rest of the troops will be kept in readiness to march at a moment's warning.

One Subaltern, one Serjeant, one Corporal, one Drummer, and twenty privates, to be left by each Corps for the security of their respective encampments. Any man who shall quit his rank on any pretence, or shall dare to plunder, or to Pillage, will be executed without mercy. (19)

The Pioneers of the Army to parade Immediately and March to the South Battery where they will Obey such orders as they will receive from Lt. Colonel Cleaveland.

By eleven o'clock, British infantry and artillery companies were parading brilliantly down Tremont Street. Many years later, witnesses to this spectacular scene still recalled this grandeur on the streets of Boston.

The Redcoats were massed together presenting a magnificent sight in all their splendor. Scarlet Redcoats were everywhere. The Redcoats were proudly marching through the town of Boston to execute a soldier's duty as ordered by General Thomas Gage. Excited children were running alongside the Redcoat warriors. The sounds of their marching boots affirmed their anger. Their anger reverberated back from the old cobblestone-streets of Boston. The British were finally attempting to breakout of Boston to end this awful siege which these guttersnipe Americans had imposed upon them. The British finally had enough of uncertainty, humiliation and rotten salt-pork. Perhaps soon, maybe soon, they would be able to go back home to their beloved island nation.

Each regiment displayed two banners on ten-foot-long staffs. On each staff were the King's Colors, along with regimental colors and numbers embroidered upon it. The Redcoats marched four abreast in perfect parade-formation. Their scarlet coats were embellished with bright, white cross-straps and shining brass-buckles. These buckles would become targets for the sharpshooting American-militiamen. The drummers wore yellow jackets. The Regulars or ordinary infantrymen wore white laced three cornered-hats. The tallest men in these regiments, the Grenadiers, appeared even taller with their high bearskin-caps. High on the neck of all the officers was a crescent-shaped silver-gorget which shone brightly in the midday sun. These glittering gorgets also made British officers prime targets for the crack shot Americans.

Even at this late hour, the Redcoats were still exuberantly taunting the Americans. Their drums were beating and their fifes were playing to the tune of *Yankee Doodle*.

"Father and I went down to camp
Along with Captain Goodwin,
And there we saw the men and boys
As thick as hasty puddin'
Yankee Doodle keep it up,
Yankee Doodle dandy,
Mind the music and the step,
And with the girls be handy."

The Redcoats continued their march. They passed the Granary Burial Ground to Queen Street, then directly onto King Street (now State Street) and past the Town House (today known as the Old State House). The Redcoats proceeded past the Customs House and finally to Long Wharf and the North Battery. At the waterfront they waited for embarkation to the Charlestown Heights.

Although the British troops looked splendid in their brilliant uniforms, they were also pitifully dressed for the scorching day and the forthcoming battle. In addition to their muskets and ammunition, each soldier was burdened with a heavy knapsack of provisions. These supplies were intended to last for three days. The whole scene was a sight to behold, as bayonets attached to muskets glistened in the sunshine. This splendid military-spectacle would continue as the Redcoats were ferried across Boston Harbor to Moulton's Point in Charlestown. (20)

The Crossing

By noontime the Redcoats were patiently waiting for their barges. Across the water in the distance, frantic activity could be discerned upon the heights of Charlestown. This activity was the New England militiamen still trying to fortify their hastily-built fortifications. Since midnight and all throughout the early morning-hours, these brave Americans were hurriedly building and molding their native soil for life saving protection against these foreign invaders. It was now one of the hottest days of the year. Hundreds of British troops would soon commence crossing the calm water of Boston Harbor. It was a short trip of about one-third mile for the imperious army of King George III.

The Royal Navy opened fire upon the redoubt with everything they had. Their cannons were furiously bombarding the Americans. Twenty-eight transport barges shoved off from the Boston shoreline. The barges were crowded with Redcoats. Each barge held approximately 50 men. Two rows of 14 barges each plied the waters of Boston Harbor. The first two barges carried British field-pieces. The barges unloaded their troops and immediately returned for more Redcoats. On the second crossing, General Howe and about 500 infantrymen embarked for Charlestown. Approximately 1,500 infantrymen had now landed at Moulton's Point. As eluded to previously, the British plan remained simple and had two main objectives; capture the redoubt in Charlestown and secondly attack Cambridge and capture General Ward's headquarters. (21)

During the British crossing, the Royal Navy and the Copp's Hill battery continued to intensify their bombardment. Black soot was starting to permeate the air. Cannonballs were being fired every other second. Most of the British cannonballs were falling short of the American redoubt. They harmlessly smacked into Breed's Hill. A few balls kept rolling and injured a several men working outside the protection of the redoubt. Unfortunately for Lt. Joseph Spaulding, he was not as lucky as the other injured men. Lt. Spaulding was working nearby the redoubt when he was hit. He tragically became the second patriot to be decapitated. Gruesomely for Colonel Prescott; he was close enough to Lt. Spaulding that some of Spaulding's remains were splattered upon the fearless colonel. Colonel Prescott calmly cleaned himself as best that he could and continued to encourage his men from the top of the parapet.

The Redcoats Arrive

The First and Second Battalions of Royal Marines, along with the following regiments participated in the Battle of Bunker Hill: The entire 5th, 38th, 43rd, 47th and 52nd Regiments, elements of the 4th, 10th, 18th, 22nd, 23rd, 35th, 59th and 63rd Regiments of Foot, along with the two companies of the famous 23rd Infantry of Welsh Fusiliers. The remaining British troops, the 49th and 64th Regiments of Foot and the 17th Light Dragoons were kept at Boston Common in readiness to march at a moment's notice. (22)

With visions of an easy British victory, young men from Essex and Kent, Northumberland and Cornwall; from Sussex to the East Midlands and Wales, from the Scottish Highlands to the green rolling-hills of Ireland, the men who hailed from the cities of Edinburgh, Swansea, Manchester, Liverpool, London, Glasgow, Plymouth, Bristol, Dublin, Cardiff, Westminster and many more towns and villages, all dreamt of returning home. They might return home, but only after their gruesome duty in America was over and done with.

The Redcoats disembarked at Moulton's Point. Adjacent to Moulton's Point is Moulton's Hill. It is the third and smallest of the hills on the Charlestown Peninsula. Moulton's Hill rose barely thirty-five feet high. It was along this small hill and the adjacent stretch of shoreline behind it that General Howe deemed it safe enough for his troops to disembark and assemble prior to the battle.

They were ordered by General Howe to have supper. They sat down on the ground and ate their bread and boiled beef. Unlike their American enemies they would be fighting on a full stomach.

During General Howe's water crossing, he noticed a large number of Americans on top of Bunker Hill. All at once, the Americans started to run down the northeast side of Bunker Hill to an area at the top of the bluffs near the beach. This quick maneuver by the Americans was made with the hope of stopping General Howe from any flanking movement to the American left. The men that General Howe saw running down Bunker Hill was Colonel John Stark and the New Hampshire troops. General Howe immediately sent word back to General Gage to release the British reinforcements. General Howe's troop strength now stood at 2,300 men and more would be arriving soon.

Suddenly, General Pigot appeared and approached General Howe with several other Redcoats. They were cursing and shouting at five unarmed British soldiers being led at the point of bayonets. Alarmed, General Howe asked, "What is this?" General Pigot answered, "Deserters sir. They broke out of ranks and ran for the American lines." Sternly General Howe said to the very frightened men, "The morning orders said, any man who shall quit his rank on any pretense will be executed without mercy. You knew this?" Quietly and without words, each man shook his head yes. "I would like to hang all five of you. But we need men. Hang those two." He randomly selected two men in the middle and they quickly fell to their knees to beseech Howe for mercy. It was a sad pathetic-scene. Discipline had to be kept and a price had to be paid for desertion. The two wayward Redcoats were hung at the nearest clump of trees and were left to dangle there all day.

Lack of American Preparations

On top of Breed's Hill, at the American redoubt, Colonel Prescott witnessed the entire British force landing at Moulton's Point. He ordered artillery officers Captain Samuel Gridley and Captain John Callender to take two cannons "to go and oppose them." He ordered Captain Thomas Knowlton to take two-hundred of his Connecticut men to support the field pieces. They ran down Breed's Hill to an open area at the end of the breastwork. They were now standing at the base of Bunker Hill. They were confused as to exactly where they were supposed to go. At the end of the breastwork, there was a gap of two-hundred yards to the bluffs which overlooked the Mystic River beach. Is this where they were supposed to be? Perhaps. Captain Knowlton wasn't sure where he was supposed to position his troops. The witless artillerists didn't seem to know where to go either. It was the fog of war settling comfortably upon the Americans and creating some early confusion at the battle site.

From the top of Bunker Hill, General Israel Putnam also observed the British troops landing at Moulton's Point. Shortly afterwards, he witnessed Captain Knowlton and his men running down the north side of Breed's Hill to the base of Bunker Hill. He rode his horse to the base of Bunker Hill and met Captain Knowlton. He ordered him to march his men a little further toward an existing rail-fence. General Putnam knew that the British would try to flank the Americans at this unoccupied position. This area also bordered a swamp close to the beach. Once there, Captain Knowlton's men began fortifying an existing rail-fence with anything they could find. They ripped apart smaller fences. They gathered stones and tall grass to plug any existing holes in the fence. They did their best to fortify this rail fence to protect themselves from musket fire. They were now about one-hundred yards to the rear of the redoubt. Unquestionably the rail fence would later prove to be an extremely valuable position for the Americans to have occupied. It would be at the rail fence that the Connecticut men would fight gallantly during the battle.

Meanwhile in a stealthy manner, the artillerists who had been with Captain Knowlton had completely disappeared. Captain Samuel Gridley and Captain John Callender were dragging their cannons back over the western slope of Bunker Hill. They were running away and deserting their duties. In short time they were found by General Israel Putnam. General Putnam ordered the artillerists to stop and go back to the redoubt. He asked them where were they going. Captain Callender said he was retreating. "On whose orders?" Putnam asked. "My own. We have no cartridges," replied Callender. General Putnam didn't believe his words. He dismounted and checked the artillery boxes and found an ample supply of cartridges and cannon-shot. "Old Put" pulled out his pistol and pointed it at Captain Callender's head. The artillerists still refused to return to the redoubt. General Putnam threatened them with death. They finally complied with his orders and reluctantly returned to their position.

Within only a few minutes and amazingly for a second time, the cunning artillerists abandoned their post. This time they left their cannons for somebody else to fire. General Putnam then ordered men from

Captain John Ford's company of Colonel Bridge's Regiment to haul the cannons back to the rail fence. The craven artillerists, Captain Callender and Captain Gridley were absolutely determined to leave the scene of the imminent battle intact. They succeeded in doing exactly that. They proceeded to desert their brethren; however, they were not the only Americans to desert the American cause on June 17, 1775.

At approximately the same time that the poltroon artillerists were deserting again; Colonel Prescott dispatched some of his best men to go into town to flank General Pigot's troops. Lt. Colonel John Robinson and Major Henry Woods of Colonel Prescott's Middlesex County Regiment, each with a detachment of men advanced down the southern slope of Breed's Hill into the burning and smoldering town. Colonel Prescott later commented that he didn't know where they went or what they did. But he was confident that they behaved with prudence and courage.

Charlestown had been set on fire from British warships, along with the Copp's Hill battery and some of the disembarked First Royal Marines. The town was lit on fire for the dual purposes that maybe the smoke might cover the advance of the British troops and also to dislodge any patriots that may have been lurking in the deserted city.

Just as several high-ranking British officers were attempting to position their men in the right place, General Putnam was trying to visualize the expected moves of the enemy. He was attempting to make sense of the unfolding British battlefield-maneuvers taking place in front of him. The experienced and savvy "Old Put" most assuredly had a good idea of what was about to happen next.

General Putnam was now back on top of Bunker Hill. He had previously been trying to organize and urge some Massachusetts men to build more fortifications. Many of these men were part of the group that had left the redoubt with the entrenching tools. He had virtually no success building fortifications with these men. They had rendered themselves useless. General Putnam attempted to gather more men for the task.

General Putnam then departed Bunker Hill for Cambridge to once again plead for more troops. He rode back to Cambridge at a gallop. With his absence, the men on top of Bunker Hill completely stopped working if they were working at all. They were all watching in amazement as the grand British military-assemblage took place in front of them. Some of these men started to desert. Fear was in the air. Only a handful of men picked up their muskets and joined the Connecticut troops at the rail fence. Colonel Prescott's premonition about these men was correct.

Colonel Prescott was doing his best to allay the fears of the men who were still with him in the redoubt. His staunch leadership was absolutely pivotal at this juncture in time. Colonel Prescott had lost many men who left the redoubt due to fatigue and desertion; but he also lost a sizable number of men who were more than willing to carry just one shovel or pickaxe back up to Bunker Hill. He had also sent some of his men out to secure other positions along the rail fence and eventually to where else he did not know. Colonel Prescott later said, "maybe as little as 150 men were left inside the redoubt." Colonel Prescott was contending with soldiers who were becoming understandably unsteady in their reasoning because of fear. It was imperative for Colonel Prescott, at this crucial time, that the potential of mass desertion be thwarted. He tried to calm them by telling them to be steady and wait to fire upon the enemy, but only on his command.

One man by the name of Peter Brown said,

"Then we saw our danger, being against eight ships of the line, and all Boston fortified against us. The danger we were in made us think there was treachery, and that we were brought there to be all slain. And I must and will say that there was treachery, oversight or presumption in the Conduct of our officers."

Peter Brown continued to expound that numerous men had deserted because of the hazard they found themselves in. The men were completely fatigued, hungry and thirsty and some of them didn't want to fight the British. Many men simply had enough of playing soldier. The incessant fog of war had led them to the sidelines.

The words from Peter Brown are powerful. He was disillusioned, frightened and very distraught. As Brown states in his own words, everybody was hungry, thirsty, weary and scared. But to his credit, Peter Brown kept working and obeyed orders. He fought bravely at Bunker Hill.

Was the American leadership making mistakes? Yes, plenty of them. The miscalculations made by the American leadership were very bad indeed. On behalf of the American plight; the engrossing fog of war would make many appearances at the Battle of Bunker Hill.

The apprehension and fear felt by the Americans was anything but palatable by the early afternoon. And their British cousins, like the good soldiers which they were, had little alternative but to believe in the wisdom of their commanding officers. If General Howe ordered his men to march straight up a hill and into a hail storm of lead, no Redcoat would question the motives of why they were doing that. They had no choice but to obey orders. There is no doubt that the British were simply excellent soldiers.

For both the Americans and the British; the Battle of Bunker Hill brought together divergent reasons why men on either side would find themselves fighting against each other on June 17, 1775. The Battle of Bunker Hill would become an earth-shattering battle for the British Empire. For each American-warrior, the Battle of Bunker Hill would further their collective-quest of throwing off the yoke of the British crown. Would the Americans remain colonial British-subjects? Or would they emerge victoriously as free citizens of a new American state?

The concept of fighting for freedom didn't need to be explained to any of the American patriots of African ancestry. They too were ready to face the British onslaught. Prominent African-American patriots who fought at Bunker Hill from Colonel Prescott's Regiment were; Peter Salem and at least two other patriots, Caesar Bason and Cuffee Whittemore. Other Massachusetts Regiments soldiered more African-American patriots like, Caleb Howe who was from Plymouth and Titus Colburn, Alexander Ames and Barzillai Lew of Andover. Also, from Massachusetts came, Caesar Bailey Dickinson, Pompey Blackman (aka Fortune/Freeman), Cuff Chambers and Samson Coburn. From Connecticut came the brother patriots, John Ashbow and Samuel Ashbow. A New Hampshire patriot by the name of Jude Hall fought at the battle. There were more than one-hundred African-Americans who are known to have fought for freedom at the Battle of Bunker Hill. Unfortunately, most of their names have been lost to history.

Several First Nation Americans fought at the Battle of Bunker Hill. Two patriot men, whose names are known to us, are; Joseph Paugenit who served in Colonel John Nixon's Regiment. He hailed from Framingham, Massachusetts and Jonathan Occum from New London, Connecticut. Occum served in General Israel Putnam's Connecticut Regiment.

(**Author's Note:** Peter Salem is variously known as Salem Poor or Salem Prince. Each name has been used and written in different accounts of the Battle of Bunker Hill. The author chooses to use the most common version of his name, Peter Salem. Salem later received a commendation from the Massachusetts General Court for his bravery at Bunker Hill.)

Moulton's Point

At Moulton's Point General Howe ordered his troops to start mustering. Officers formed their companies and companies became regiments. Three thousand British troops were now in Charlestown. The British were readying themselves to do battle with the progeny of people who had left their beloved island of Britain generations ago. The combatant forces were family. The Americans and the British were cousins. The dismal situation on the Charlestown Peninsula was sorrowful for both the Americans and British. Many men were about to be killed or severely wounded. Each side would suffer terribly. It was a sad day for both the Americans and the British. Familial ties didn't seem to matter very much anymore. The worst of a family quarrel had appeared. This quarrel would continue to be played out on the heights of Charlestown, at the Battle of Bunker Hill.

Before the battle, General Howe had something to say to his men;

"Gentlemen, -I am very happy in having the honor of commanding so fine a body of men: I do not in the least doubt but that you will behave like Englishmen, and as becometh good soldiers.

If the enemy will not come from their intrenchments, we must drive them out, at all events, otherwise the town of Boston will be set on fire by them.

I shall not desire one of you to go a step further than where I go myself at your head.

Remember, gentlemen, we have no recourse to any resources if we lose Boston, but to go on board our ships, which will be very disagreeable to us all." (23)

Prior to the British formations marching out to meet the Americans in battle, some American reinforcements had finally arrived at the redoubt and the breastwork. A conglomeration of men from the Massachusetts Regiments of Colonel Jonathan Brewer, Colonel John Nixon, Colonel Moses Little, Colonel Benjamin Woodbridge and Major Willard Moore, were a welcomed relief for those already there. It was these men who built the three small-fleches, in a precarious open area, between the end of the breastwork and the rail fence to help support the American left.

In a very short time, Colonel William Prescott and his remaining Massachusetts men in the earthen redoubt, along the breastwork and the small fleches; together with General Israel Putnam who furiously rode around the American lines, with Captain Thomas Knowlton commanding his Connecticut troops at the rail fence, all of these skilled patriots were in position and ready to do battle. Colonel John Stark, Major Andrew McClary and Captain Henry Dearborn and their New Hampshire troops were at the stone wall, the Mystic River beach and also in positions along the rail fence. Major General John Thomas and General Nathanael Greene were ready with their troops at the Boston Neck holding the American line. Finally, General Artemus Ward and Major General Dr. Joseph Warren were in command at the American headquarters in Cambridge. They were also ready for a fight. All of these American warriors, with their rank-and-file, would soon be answering General William Howe's prophetic words.

By 3 p.m. it had already been fifteen long-hours for the toiling Americans. They had gone without any food and little to drink since midnight. They were scared, tired, hungry and thirsty. When reinforcements finally arrived; the men were beseeched by their wanting brethren for any victuals. Yet, many men received no relief. The battle was imminent.

The day slipped deeper into the danger zone coaxed by the fog of war.

Upon hearing the British cannonading, Major General Dr. Joseph Warren knew exactly where he belonged and that was with his men at Bunker Hill. He left the safety of General Ward's headquarters and started to walk. Along the road, Dr. Joseph Warren found a patriot that gave him his horse. Dr. Joseph Warren rode swiftly to Charlestown. There he witnessed hundreds of Americans frozen in fear. He ascended up Bunker Hill and received a musket from the wounded Lt. Colonel Dr. James Brickett. Shortly afterward, General Putnam found Dr. Warren. General Putnam was in the midst of his endless mission to build a fortification on top of Bunker Hill and continued to direct men to critical positions. General Putnam offered Dr. Warren his command. Dr. Warren refused. Dr. Warren then asked "Old Put" where he could be best put to use. General Putnam told him to go to the redoubt. Dr. Warren then went down to the redoubt and the same exact conversation took place between Dr. Warren and Colonel Prescott. Colonel Prescott offered to relinquish his command to him. Again Dr. Warren refused. He told Colonel Prescott he was there as a volunteer because he hadn't officially received his commission as a major general. He then asked to be directed to where he could be of best use. Colonel Prescott told him to find a place in the line with the men along the redoubt walls. This is exactly where Dr. Warren wanted to be. He then took his place among his fellow patriots to defeat the foreign invaders.

More significant American-leadership arrived in time to battle the Red-coats. General Seth Pomeroy arrived from his Northampton home, after riding nearly one full-day and one-hundred miles. He was carrying his old musket which he had made three decades earlier. When General Pomeroy arrived at the Charlestown Neck, he dismounted and sent his borrowed horse back to Cambridge for the safety of the steed. He walked the last half-mile up Bunker Hill and reported to General Putnam. He told Putnam he was volunteering his services. He said he didn't want any type of com-mand, echoing the request made by Major General Dr. Joseph Warren. General Putnam proceeded to send General Seth Pomeroy to do battle along the rail fence.

General Pomeroy was a steadying influence to the Americans. He was a military legend in Massachusetts. Some of the patriots at the rail fence, were carrying weapons which were made by General Pomeroy. These pa-triot warriors were very glad indeed to see this esteemed man. When General Pomeroy arrived at the rail fence, he purportedly said,

"You see this gun?" "Thirty years ago, to this very day, I was carrying it at Louisbourg when the French surrendered. We beat the French Regu-lars without any help from the British that day. We'll do the same thing to the Redcoats today."

General Seth Pomeroy was exactly the type of leader which the Amer-icans needed at the battle. This brave man provided essential leadership at the right moment and at the right time.

Another prominent volunteer was James Otis. This great American or-ator was one of the first men to publicly help ignite the notions of American liberty and freedom. Sadly, Otis was incapacitated for a lot of his adult life. He suffered from mental deficiencies that started in the 1760's. His condition worsened after he received a severe blow to his head in a fight with British tax collector John Robinson. Robinson hit Otis with his cudgel at the British Coffee House in 1769. He survived the Battle of Bunker Hill.

There was additional encouragement for the patriots at the rail fence in the form of two cannons. The men cheered a loud huzzah when Captain Samuel Trevett arrived. He had dragged his two small-cannons all the way from Cambridge and then up and over Bunker Hill. He managed to fire them several times at the Redcoats.

The American patriots all along their advanced positions were now as ready as they would ever be. In short time, they would be fighting for their lives that embodied their values of liberty, freedom, unalienable rights, democracy, opportunity and equality.

At Moulton's Point Major General William Howe divided his forces into two divisions. The first division of Redcoats would consist of the light infantry, the Grenadiers and the 5th and 52nd Regiments. General Howe would personally command these troops. General Howe would be on the British right-wing, on the American left. He planned to smash through the American line at the rail fence. He would cut off any retreat from the redoubt. The second division consisted of the 38th, 43rd, 47th Regiments and the First Battalion of Royal Marines, which were under the command of General Sir Robert Pigot. General Pigot commanding on the British left-wing, was ordered to break through to the breastwork and strike into the redoubt.

General Howe's plans were uncomplicated and straightforward. According to his own presumptions and those of the British high-command, this battle would not last long. Most importantly to General Thomas Gage and to General William Howe, the bedrock doctrine of their plan was unambiguous; the Americans would either quickly surrender or just run away as fast as they could. The British would be in Cambridge by nightfall.

Parading Forth With Pomp and Ceremony

From Moulton's Point at 3:30 p.m., with precision, pomp and ceremonial display; the British Regulars marched in locked cadence toward their American enemy. Their regimental colors were proudly held high and were waving in the bright sunshine. Shoulder to shoulder, British troops from far across the Atlantic ocean, were slowly approaching the redoubt. But the Redcoats were burdened by the weight of their knapsacks. Their knapsacks were full of provisions. They weighed at least 60 pounds. Some historians have claimed that the Redcoats carried close to 125 pounds strapped on their backs. Whatever the true weight of a Redcoat knapsack was, there is little doubt that they were too heavy and burdensome for battle. Furthermore, the Redcoats were expected to fight with their backpacks and not discard them before attacking. The advancing Redcoats also faced other impediments. They were hindered by the tall uncut-grass that hid approximately a dozen-rows of stoutly-built fences. These tall fences had strong posts and railings. They couldn't easily be dismantled. Cumbersomely the British struggled to go around them. These barriers continually delayed their progress. They were also stymied by the never-ending uneven ground. There were clumps of trees to go around. Brick kilns were in the way. There was miry ground to navigate. The midafternoon sun exasperated their discomfort. It was a hot day for the month of June and the Redcoats were already suffering terribly.

Upon the British commencement to battle, Colonel Prescott continued to encourage his men. He fearlessly roamed the top of the parapet. All of his senior and junior officers resolutely mirrored Colonel Prescott's words. They repeated them over and over.

Colonel Prescott said, "Powder is scarce and must not be wasted. Fire low. Aim at the waistbands. Wait until you see the white of their eyes. Aim at the handsome coats. Pick off the commanders." (24)

Only minutes away from battle, Colonel Prescott was trying to make those last few minutes count with encouragement and assurances of victory. He was insuring his men with a calm, steady and guiding demeanor.

"Steady now boys. Take sure aim. Find the officers and drop them. Make every shot count. Hit your mark. Listen to my commands. Don't fire until told to do so. Look at 'em shine in the sun my boys! They're just walking targets. Hold steady. Aim at the officers. Aim at their handsome coats. Fire low. Don't over-shoot. We'll show them what we can do. You're all marksmen and there's not one of you that can't kill a squirrel at one-hundred yards. Reserve your fire and we will destroy every one of them. Pick off the commanders."

These words of encouragement were spoken frequently by all the officers along the American line. Patriot Philip Johnson testified that he distinctly heard General Putnam utter the momentous and legendary words;

"Men, you are all marksmen. Don't one of you fire until you see the white of their eyes!" (25)

The Carnage On the Beach

On the British far right, General Howe sent eleven companies of light infantry to destroy Colonel Stark's men behind the stone wall. These noteworthy companies were comprised of four different regiments. These particular Redcoats were the cream of the British Army. The Welsh Fusiliers, the King's Own Regiment, the 10th Foot Regiment and the 52nd Foot Regiment were ordered to rid the Mystic River beach of these revolutionaries. Once the Redcoats defeated the Americans rebels on the small-beach, they would continue their flanking movement up and over the bluffs to reach the rail fence. General Howe ordered his six-pound field pieces to open fire upon the patriots. However, the British artillerists couldn't even begin to fire their bombardment. Why? Amazingly, General Gage's chief artillerist, Lt. Colonel Samuel Cleveland was pursuing his romantic endeavors in Boston. He was flirting with the schoolmaster's daughters. Cleveland was simply absent without leave and disregarding his duties. He had sent over to Charlestown, twelve-pound balls instead of the needed six-pounders for the smaller cannons. Thanks to Cleveland's incompetence, there would be no artillery fire raining down upon the Americans on the beach. One officer wrote about Cleveland and said,

"The wretched blunder of the over-sized balls sprung from the dotage of an officer, of rank in the Corps, who spends his time dallying with schoolmaster John Lovell's daughters."

To compound his artillery problems, General Howe couldn't use his twelve-pound cannons either. This was because of the marshy and muddy ground. This unknown pitfall stopped his cannons from being moved by the artillerists. They were stopped cold in their tracks. The cannons sat there totally useless. This part of General Howe's battle plan had failed terribly and was a portent of the coming battle. The fog of war was firmly intrenched and greeting the British once again.

The Redcoats continued their march along the narrow beach. They were marching four abreast and ready to do battle with the American rebels. General Howe surmised that Colonel Stark's men would only have enough time to fire perhaps just one volley; then they would run away from the fourteen-inch bayonets coming toward them. The British rank-and-file were experts at using this terrifying blade. They were exclusively ordered to make a bayonet charge and not to fire upon the Americans. Why would the British want to withhold their fire? Why would such an order be given to the Redcoats? The British simply believed in their blades and the age-old tactic of a running charge at the enemy. General Howe knew that at least one volley would be fired at his men. He also knew that some of his men would be slaughtered, but he believed his Redcoats would prevail. The rank-and-file Redcoats were merely fodder to be used as the command saw fit. The Redcoats continued onward as they marched closer and closer to the stone wall.

Colonel Stark employed a strategy that perhaps General Howe wasn't aware of or expecting. Years earlier when Colonel Stark was a young officer in the British Colonial Militia and under the command of the outstanding military-leader Robert Rogers; Colonel Stark had learned a few useful tricks about eighteenth-century military-tactics. He had personally used these tactics in the French and Indian War. These were the tactics which Colonel Stark employed on the Mystic River beach.

Colonel Stark hammered a stick into the sand. It was forty-yards from the stone wall. This marker indicated the distance that Colonel Stark wanted his men to withhold their fire until the Redcoats arrived. The patriots would then be given the order to fire. With precision movements and strict discipline, Colonel Stark had prepared his men well. The Americans would be deployed three rows deep on the beach. This formation allowed the first row of kneeling men to fire and then reload. The second row of patriots, stooping behind the first row, would fire and then they too would reload. This tactic was subsequently repeated by the third-row, who carefully fired from behind the second row of men. The American round-robin of firing their weapons would continue over and over again. The net result of this strategy was; there would be a constant and continuous fire from the Americans dropping the oncoming Redcoats. Colonel Stark's strategy worked exactly as planned.

The young men from the west of Britain had finally reached the marker in the sand. There was no turning back for the Welsh Fusiliers and only seconds to live. A one-word command filled the ears of the patriots. Fire! The loudest noise that any of them had ever heard in their life permeated the scene. The carnage had begun! Bang! A second round was fired! The crashing thunder of American muskets filled the air and their muskets filled the Redcoats with lead. The British started to drop. They dropped dead or dropped severely-wounded. The Welsh Fusiliers incredibly and bravely proceeded to regroup and started to advance again. They were walking over their dead, dying and severely wounded-countrymen. The cries of anguish filled the air. Bang! A third volley burst forth from the patriot muskets. Again, more Redcoats fell. Stunned and completely dazed while enveloped in their ghastly plight, the remaining half-dozen Welsh Fusiliers now watched as the King's Own Regiment tried their hand at attacking the Americans behind the stone wall.

The King's Own Regiment, in their apparent haste to die, rushed past the wounded and dying Welsh Fusiliers. Perhaps some of the men from the King's Own Regiment believed they would meet the same fate as the Welshmen. They would have been correct. These brave soldiers willingly met the same demise as the Welsh Fusiliers. Bang! American muskets fired again. For a fourth time, British troops fell into a tangled heap of dead, dying and severely wounded-men. The carnage on the beach quickly doubled and then it tripled with fallen Redcoats. A continuous sheet of flames and a thunderous roar of musket fire was followed by a hail storm of molten lead. American musketballs tore apart the British warriors. The one-ounce musketballs were devastating, as British bones were smashed apart and large chunks of flesh were torn out. American musketballs tore out entire muscles from the arms and legs of the enemy. The Americans were now firing and reloading their muskets as fast as they could. It was a ruckus moment for the Americans. It was a moment of bedlam and carnage for the British. It was an ongoing scene of bloodshed. It was annihilation on the beach!

Now it was the turn of the 10th Foot Regiment. After the forsaken charges against the Americans, the 10th Foot Regiment was determined to succeed and drive the Americans back. Once again, the Redcoats were stepping over their dead and dying men from the previous two failed regiments. American musketballs quickly started to drop the men of the 10th Foot Regiment. Sadly, for the Redcoats there was more carnage and even more waste of excellent soldiers. This ongoing insanity by the Redcoats, who were willing to walk into a hail storm of molten lead, had now entered the world of the bizarre. Because of his tactics, General William Howe was already heading toward complete disaster. But the British assault wasn't over yet! The fog of war wasn't through with the British on the Mystic River beach. More slaughter was in the offing!

Tragically for the rank-and-file Redcoats, it was a commonplace practice to walk into fired bullets. Why? Because they were ordered by their officers to do so. No questions were ever asked by the rank-and-file. This manner of ludicrous, wretched and shameful-fighting was the normal and stupefyingly ridiculous-tactic that all European armies of the eighteenth-century deployed. The British embraced these maniacal tactics at the Battle of Bunker Hill. The fog of war closely embraced the British.

The surviving Redcoats were laying on the beach crying out for help. Nobody came to help them. Dead Redcoats floated face down in the shallow waters of the Mystic River. The river waters slowly turned to crimson. The life blood of these brave British-soldiers oozed from their bodies into the ebb tide. The New Hampshire men watched in horror, as many of the dying and severely wounded-enemies were writhing in agony while mingled amongst their dead. The Americans stood completely intact in stunned silence. Colonel Stark and his New Hampshire marksmen were astonished at the stupidity of what they had just experienced.

There is no doubt that luck played a big role for the last surviving British Regiment on the beach. The 52nd Foot Regiment was trudging behind the Welsh Fusiliers, the King's Own Regiment and the 10th Foot Regiment. The luck of the 52nd Foot began when they were ordered to be the last regiment to plod down the Mystic River beach. After the other three regiments were decimated, it was their turn to attempt to vanquish the Americans. They too were astonished at the sight of the massacre of their fellow countrymen. Their officers were ordering the men of the 52nd Foot Regiment to commit suicide! This would be done with the help of American muskets. The rank-and-file Redcoats of the 52nd Foot knew that this was insane. They were powerless to be able to do anything about it because they had their orders! They knew that they would not be able to complete General Howe's mission orders. Suddenly the men of the 52nd Foot Regiment became extremely reluctant to follow their orders. In fact, they didn't follow orders! They stopped in their tracks. Stern and unrelenting British officers did all that they could, short of murdering their own men, to prod the Redcoats to walk into a hail storm of American musketballs. The officers struck their men with their swords. The officers cursed at them with every nasty and vile comment which could be conceived. The men balked and refused to advance! There were piles of their dead countrymen a mere 50-feet from them. The Redcoats were still falling dead on the sand! Finally, some sort of sensibility was found by the British officers. They ordered a retreat. The Redcoats quickly fled this gruesome sight of the British carnage played out on the Mystic River beach. Some of the British attempted to carry their wounded to safety. The British slaughter was compliments of the fog of war.

Reverend Peter Thacher, watching from the north shore of the Mystic River in Chelsea, described the British retreat from the beach. He recounted that he observed the light infantry, "in very great disorder down to the point where they landed, and there some of them even into their boats; at this time their officers were observed by spectators on the opposite side of the shore to use the most passionate gestures and even to push forward ye men with their swords."

The British utterly failed with their foray upon the Mystic River beach. They were completely slaughtered. For all their troubles; they left behind

96 dead soldiers and many were severely wounded. Colonel John Stark commented about the British fiasco. He proclaimed after the battle,

"I never saw sheep lie as thick in the fold."

As the decimated British ran away the Americans let out a big huzzah. They had defeated the vaunted British Redcoats on the small Mystic River beach. The Battle of Bunker Hill was still in its early stages and quickly unfolding. The British slaying on the beach was only one-segment of a long, hot and stupefying-day.

General William Howe had already begun his attack on the rail fence, when a messenger arrived with the disastrous news of the British rout on the beach. Instantly General Howe's plan to flank the Americans from the bluffs was shattered. Perhaps his plan to sleep in Cambridge that night had also vanished for him. Whatever might transpire from this point forward, one aspect was certain, uncertainty now reigned for General Howe. General Howe's realization of being driven from Massachusetts would play a major role in any future battlefield decisions.

How did the British rout on the beach happen? Apparently General William Howe didn't completely think through his failed-strategy. The fog of war certainly followed his troops directly onto the Mystic River beach. The fog of war helped to create this disastrous-outcome and the senseless-slaughter of British soldiers. General Howe was shocked and he couldn't afford any more perilous errors.

General Howe now clearly understood that there was no alternative but victory at Bunker Hill. If he couldn't prevail and "win the day" for the crown, then back to Boston he would have to retreat. If he couldn't prevail, then the British would have to flee from the shores of Massachusetts. General William Howe was in a place of no return and he knew it.

The First Attack On the Hill

The small American-redoubt on Breed's Hill was finally finished. The three small-fleches were also completed. Colonel Prescott was trying to bridge the gap between the redoubt and the breastwork that ran toward the rail fence with the three small-fleches. There was nothing more that could be done. The enemy was advancing along a wide open-area.

Colonel Prescott was still defying death. Once more he jumped on top of the parapet and made a spectacle of himself. He was a conspicuous target. Colonel Prescott kicked up the muzzles of patriot muskets, as he moved along the top of the redoubt. He was warning his men not to fire until ordered to do so. He told them that none of the Redcoats would enter their redoubt if they kept disciplined and listened to his commands.

To the American left there was a double battle-line of advancing Redcoats. It stretched halfway across the Charlestown Peninsula. Ten companies marched side by side in parade formation. With their sleek scarlet uniforms and bayonets glistening in the radiating sun; some of these Redcoat warriors were taking their last steps for their king and country.

To the immediate south of the redoubt at the bottom of Breed's Hill, the once picturesque village of Charlestown was now in flames. This terrible conflagration was taking its toll. Nearly 400 homes, businesses, churches and other structures were burning to the ground. The total cost of the destruction of Charlestown was, £117,982 5s. 2d. (26)

Yet within the deserted village there were approximately 300 American-militiamen. They were attempting to menace and flank General Pigot's Redcoats or at the very least slow him down. As the Redcoats advanced the Americans fought them from house to house. American snipers were successfully dropping the advancing Redcoats. Once pressed, the patriots would simply fall back to another strategic-position. The Americans were quick to regain any territory if the situation presented itself.

While the running battle in Charlestown was taking place, Vice Admiral Graves made a token appearance to consult with General Howe. It was a useless endeavor. Up to this point Vice Admiral Graves had nominally supported General Howe's efforts. Once again, he rebuffed General Howe's request to send a warship to the Mystic River. Vice Admiral Graves was lazy and his obstinance had no boundaries. He didn't even bother to take sounding measurements of the Mystic River. Instead of sending a warship, Graves ordered floating-batteries to make their way to the north side of the peninsula. This would be a slow effort because of the lack of wind. The gondolas would have to be rowed against the emerging ebb tide. This would take too long to benefit General Howe's troops. The final result of this pointless consultation was the fog of war had reintroduced itself to Vice Admiral Graves and his Royal Navy.

General Johnny Burgoyne who fired upon Charlestown from Copp's Hill in Boston, had this comment about the wanton destruction of the seaside town;

"To consider this action as a soldier, it comprised, though in a small compass, almost every branch of military duty and curiosity. Whole streets of houses, ships upon the stocks, a number of churches, all sending up volumes of smoke and flame, or falling together in ruins, were capital objects. A prospect of the neighboring hills, the steeples of Boston, and the masts of such ships as were employed in the harbor, all crowded with spectators, friends and foes alike in anxious suspense, made a background to the piece; and the whole together composed a representation of war that I think the imagination of Lebrun never reached."

To the north of the burning town the Redcoats were approaching slowly up the eastern slope of Breed's Hill. Numerous impediments were in the way. British lines broke and reformed several times because of unseen fences. There were also overgrown clumps of tall-grass in many places and numerous potholes. Several kilns and a lot of sludgy ground had to be navigated. Despite all of these hindrances, General Howe was bravely and gallantly leading his men. He told them that he would not ask them to go where he would not venture to go first. He was out in front of all his men as he said he would be. He was keeping true to his word and leading by example. Marching alongside of him were his twelve staff-officers. However, because General Howe was involved with the moment-to-moment direction of his division on the British right; he effectively lost control and contact with the British division on his left. General Pigot was leading the left division of Redcoats and now was effectively on his own. General Pigot was now commanding these regiments; the 5th, 38th, 43rd, 47th, 52nd and the Royal Marines commanded by Major John Pitcairn. General Howe had his hands full and was completely occupied with his own command. General Howe was not aware of what General Pigot was doing or the current circumstances in which he was operating. In essence, there was no overall British battlefield commander. Inadvertently General Howe took himself out of that position while trying to control his own division. The fog of war stealthily helped guide him into this predicament.

The Americans from the very start of the day had no overall battlefield commander. General Putnam attempted to fill this role; however, he wasn't in charge of all the troops and was aware of his command limitations regarding men from other colonies. He was only in command of the Connecticut troops. There were times when feisty General Putnam felt the need to threaten men from other colonies into action. Even then, men disregarded him as he tried to coordinate troops from atop his horse. He was nominally in command at the rail fence, but he wasn't in command at the breastwork. He wasn't in command on the Mystic River beach. He definitely wasn't in command at the redoubt. The only battlefield position which General Putnam was totally in command of was at the top of Bunker Hill. Nothing of any critical significance was happening on top of Bunker Hill, except for dozens of useless malingering-militiamen who were watching in awe as the battle progressed. These ineffectual militiamen were doing nothing else except being quite insubordinate to their orders. As previously stated, and quite lamentably for the American cause, men from another colony frequently didn't comply or legally have to obey the orders of an officer from a different colony. This was the sad plight of American leadership at the Battle of Bunker Hill. The fog of war continuously swirled around and around the Americans.

General Putnam was determined to lead by example. Captain John Ford had hauled Captain John Callender's two cannons into position between the rail fence and the breastwork. General Putnam proceeded to fire them. His first few shots were not even close to the Redcoats and they splashed into Boston Harbor. Without an experienced artillerist to help fire the cannons, General Putnam did his best. There were also no accoutrements for him, such as a sponge or a wormer to clean the cannons. In frustration, he managed to split one of the cannons down its side when he heaved himself upon it while in a fit of fury.

General Putnam did have some success with the remaining big-gun but only after he had corrected its position. He rammed powder down its muzzle and filled it with nearly three-hundred musketballs. General Putnam in his customary way then cursed at the enemy. He fired at the Grenadiers just as they were reforming because a brick kiln was in their way. General Putnam succeeded in tearing apart the ranks of these Redcoats. Some of the patriots nearby cheered him on. The American field-pieces were finally becoming effective. The British soon closed ranks and started to advance once more.

Eventually a few militiamen from Colonel Moses Little's regiment answered General Putnam's call when he asked for help. "Who knows how to charge these pieces?" Privates Halliday and Dutton volunteered, along with a British deserter named Hill. Hill had some artillery experience but wasn't an expert by any measure. General Putnam then climbed on top of his old white-horse to make his customary round of American positions. As he was leaving, he said, "Fire till she melts lads." Off rode brave General Putnam. Halliday, Dutton and Hill found some solid shot and primed the cannon to fire. They fired twice but hit nothing. Hill adjusted the aim to fire lower and the next shot smashed straight through the Redcoats. The men cheered their success and with this success more patriots decided to get involved. One young man rammed a charge down the muzzle of the cannon. Tragically a flame shot out from the cannon and burned the young patriot's face. He was rushed off the battlefield. That was the last of any amateur artillerist stepping up to fire the big-gun. Consequently, the cannon sat quiet. The American fog of war had enveloped it.

As the Battle of Bunker Hill unfolded, whether it was a British or American officer; most of the officers led their men as best that they could during the confusion everybody seemed to be in. This confusion was the proverbial fog of war. It hung over the battlefield like a thunderous cloud.

The fog of war was again affecting General Howe's judgment. Uncertain of his next move, he made a hasty decision to proceed forward with his outstretched double line of infantry. General Howe did this with trepidation. His men were going to first make a bayonet charge and then hopefully clobber the Americans. Wasn't that the plan all along? But this slow motion-attack moved along ponderously. It plodded along. British progress was methodical but exceedingly slow. And sometimes, the Redcoats just stopped. They had to constantly maneuver around annoying obstacles. But they kept coming. The Redcoats were finally approaching the American line. The British were still overconfident of a victory. They were now a mere ninety-yards from the American line and hopefully soon would continue on to Cambridge by that evening.

At the rail fence, Captain Knowlton ordered his men not to fire until the Redcoats came within fifteen-rods of them. Still moving slowly, the Redcoats were now just seventy-yards away. Then there was just one-hundred-feet separating the Redcoats from the Americans. The Redcoats were attempting to smash through a tall fence when Lt. James Dana of Connecticut began firing. The firing spread all along the rail fence. Dana wanted to draw enemy fire. He succeeded. Another firefight was now underway. The Redcoats apparently were terrible shots. Their musketballs flew harmlessly over the heads of the patriots and landed mostly into some trees behind them. Captain Henry Dearborn, fighting on the extreme right of the rail fence, said, "Forty-nine out of fifty of their bullets went six feet over our heads."

The British advance stopped. Similar to the fighting on the beach, Americans simply fired their muskets and the British fell dead or wounded. Miraculously for General Howe, he remained unscathed.

Lamentably for the general, every one of his officers that were located near him had either fell dead or were badly wounded. Two of General Howe's staff were killed and ten were wounded. General Howe's naval aide, Lt. Jourdain toppled over dead, with a musketball lodged in his head and Captain George Sherwin lay dead on Breed's Hill with a chest wound. Lt. Thomas Page had his leg shattered.

In a rather strange and surreal moment on the battlefield; General Howe's valet Adjutant Evans, while pouring a glass of red wine for the general, had the wine bottle shot out of his hand. A musketball then smashed through the arm of the manservant sending him to the ground. General Howe stood there all alone with no cool wine to drink. Pity, poor General Howe. Now he had nobody to pour his battle wine. Such a pity.

Colonel Prescott later recalled seeing General Howe standing almost alone, surrounded entirely by the dead and wounded. He stood there with British blood splattered all over his once beautiful uniform. General Howe was staggered.

Many Americans at the rail fence were marksmen. Heavy American firepower was also coming from the redoubt and breastwork. Whenever a British officer was identified he immediately became a prime target for a musketball or two, or three. The ridiculous ornamental neck-gorget, which British officers wore, was the main culprit of identification by the Americans. The sunshine reflecting off the gorget proclaimed and simply spelled out; here is a British officer, shoot him! The Americans did just that. The militiamen encouraged each other to take shots at the British officers. "There's one! Let's have a shot at him!" Bang! British officers by the score fell dead in the glistening sun due to their silly ornamentation. One fallen officer was Lt. Colonel James Abercromby, the commander of the Grenadiers. As Abercromby was being carried to the rear, amazingly he was identified by the Americans. He could hear the Americans taunting him, "Colonel Abercromby are the Americans cowards now?" Abercromby died a British hero a week later in Boston.

General Howe's ten companies of Grenadiers led the way. They were followed by the 5th and 52nd Regiments. These columns of Redcoats crashed into each other because of the barriers. It was a chaotic scene for the British. The orderly life, which every British soldier was familiar with, had suddenly disappeared. There was no order on the hills of Charlestown, only chaos created by the fog of war. British lines grew thinner and thinner. Bang! Another explosion of American musket fire tore into the

Redcoats, then another and another. The Redcoats were being raked by Captain Samuel Trevett's cannon. His cannonballs ripped apart the Grenadiers. There was seemingly no end to this bloodbath. One British officer described the scene he witnessed, "As we approached, an incessant stream of fire poured from the Rebel line; it seemed a continued sheet of fire for near thirty minutes."

The battle almost became futile for the British. They broke ranks and quickly scurried out of range of American musketballs. Some of the more exuberant Americans started to give chase to the Redcoats, but were immediately ordered back by their officers. To their delight, the Americans were able to taunt the Redcoats with several loud huzzahs. The Americans were enthusiastically enjoying the moment. There were a few exceptions to the jubilation that most of the Americans were feeling. Many years later, Ralph Farnum recalled the most hideous and frightening sound of the battle for him was not the thunderous sound of hundreds of muskets, but the screams of agony from the enemy Redcoats.

Ralph Farnum claimed he was the last surviving American veteran of the Battle of Bunker Hill. When he was 105 years-old, he said the cries of the enemy was his most vivid memory. He said, "It was louder than the firearms." He confessed that he became sick before he could pull his trigger once again.

A British letter dated July 5, 1775, says: "Our light-infantry were served up in companies against the grass fence, without being able to penetrate; indeed, how could we penetrate? Most of our Grenadiers and light-infantry, the moment of presenting themselves, lost three-fourths, and many nine-tenths of their men. Some had only eight or nine men a company left; some only three, four, and five." (27)

General Howe standing alone surveyed the disaster he helped to create. He later recalled and commented how he felt at that precise moment. He said, "There was a moment I never felt before."

On the British left, General Pigot was having his own troubles. He was waiting to see what transpired with General Howe's division. The men of the 38th, 43rd and 47th Regiments and the First Battalion of Royal Marines tried to advance slowly and methodically out of Charlestown. General Pigot's men were effectively and continuously harassed by the Americans. When the British emerged from the burning village the patriots were flanking them every step of the way. General Pigot was expected to charge the redoubt, but his line started to collapse. The patriots were successfully stopping General Pigot with every attempt he made to advance. The American militiamen were doing their job and doing it well. The Americans were relentless in their attack upon him. General Pigot's advance suddenly stopped. He was stymied. Ultimately General Pigot was unable to launch an effective attack against the redoubt. He had little choice but to pull back his troops. The patriots gleefully watched the fleeing Redcoats. They were jubilant and suffered no casualties. Would the British return again? Only time would tell.

General William Howe ordered his army to regroup at the foot of the hill. He was attempting to grasp what happened. The British debacle was analogous to an unseen, prodigious steel-fist that smacked the British so hard that any recovery would only be construed as a miracle. The British were all but completely knocked out! How could this possibly happen? Wondrously, the British persevered. They were superb professional-soldiers. The reality for General Howe was, he had little choice but to continue fighting. He was planning to mount a second attack. Of General Howe's 750 light infantry and Grenadiers, 450 now lay dead and wounded on the Mystic River beach and among the tall New England-grass in front of the rail fence.

In Boston and the close neighboring-towns, patriots and loyalists alike witnessed the burning of Charlestown and the Battle of Bunker Hill. Massive pillars of fire climbed up Charlestown's church steeple. Broad columns of black smoke pushed out over Boston Harbor. The epic Battle of Bunker Hill was watched from distant roof-tops, hills and any elevated vantage point. Boston's shoreline was full of onlookers. It was a sight so abhorrent; nobody would ever forget this awesome scene or exactly where they were as witnesses many years later.

Almost eight-miles away in Braintree; from the pinnacle of Penn's Hill, a seven-year-old boy was watching the battle with his mother. Her name was Abigail Adams. The boy was John Quincy Adams, the future sixth-President of the United States. His father John Adams, the future second-President of the United States was in Philadelphia attending to his duties at the Second Continental Congress.

Twenty minutes after the first British attack, General Artemus Ward was informed the British were sending more Redcoats to Charlestown. These were General Howe's reserve troops. General Ward then countered with additional troops to Bunker Hill. The threat of an immediate assault into Cambridge had subsided for now. Among the troops General Ward sent to Bunker Hill were, Colonel Thomas Gardner's Regiment, Colonel John Patterson's Regiment and Colonel John Ward's Regiment.

Colonel Gardner had been stationed on the crest of Prospect Hill, not far from the Charlestown Neck. Within the ranks of Colonel Gardner's Regiment, a company of 45 Charlestown men were under the command of Captain Josiah Harris. From their vantage point on top of Prospect Hill, the locals had watched their homes and their beloved village of Charlestown put to the torch by the enemy. The Townies were half mad with rage and possessed no other feelings than revenge. The men of Charlestown were more than ready to do battle with these foreign invaders. The Townies weren't patient, but they waited for their orders.

Captain Josiah Harris and his Townies had not been home since April 19, 1775. On that day, they had left Charlestown to fight the British retreating from Lexington and Concord. Captain Harris asked Colonel Gardner for permission to go into battle. Colonel Gardner said no. Colonel Gardner was acting the good soldier and explained that he had not received any orders to advance into Charlestown. Again, Captain Harris asked Colonel Gardner to release his company. Once more the answer was no. Captain Harris then received the answer he wanted to hear. "Advance!" The Townies quick stepped and proceeded past the neck and onto the battlefield.

Meanwhile Colonel John Ward's troops stationed at Lechmere's Point received orders to go to Bunker Hill. They double-timed their march of less than two miles and arrived at the neck behind Colonel Gardner. Colonel Gardner's men started to advance across the neck when a mysterious rider appeared and questioned them, "Who gave you orders to advance?" "General Artemus Ward" was the reply. "The Committee of Safety countermands it." This mysterious rider then galloped away. In all the confusion nobody initially identified him. Later several men said it was the traitor Dr. Benjamin Church. The traitor Church was sowing seeds of confusion along the American lines. How could Colonel Ward know this order was bogus? He didn't. He just stood there motionless and confused, as the fog of war encircled him. He knew that the Committee of Safety had authority to issue such an order. But who was this rider? Feisty Captain Seth Washburn innately knew that this order was phony. Washburn told Colonel Ward, "I don't care who gave the order. I say it's a Tory order and we should ignore it." Without Colonel Ward, Captain Washburn then led his men across the dangerous neck. They ran as fast as they could. The neck was being raked by British naval-guns. Two other companies followed Washburn and eventually Colonel John Ward crossed over by himself leaving many men in his regiment behind.

Shortly afterward, Captain Josiah Harris and his Townies charged down from the top of Bunker Hill and took their position at the rail fence. Although the exact time of their arrival is unknown, it was probably just sometime before the second British attack.

The Calamitous Second British Attack

As British disorder was browbeaten and checked into order; British drummers bellowed out the call for the Redcoats to line up for a second assault. The Redcoats quickly and eagerly lined up. They reformed themselves with inherent British pride. General Howe was about to let loose his powerful army once more. It was now 4:00 p.m. and the British started to advance.

The patriot militiamen in the redoubt or anywhere else on the American line were still without food or water. All day long the patriots had opined for the basic needs of life. And now as expected, their powder was dangerously close to being exhausted. A few artillery cartridges were opened and the powder was distributed among the men. The current predicament that the Americans found themselves didn't need to happen. Deft American planning was woefully absent and personal responsibility was abandoned in Cambridge the prior evening. The American shortfall of necessary arms and supplies highlighted their grievous-gaffes. Pitifully there were only a handful of patriots with bayonets inside the redoubt, at the rail fence and behind the breastwork. The malicious fog of war had volunteered to orchestrate all of the American bedlam that was now running rampant.

The legendary Battle of Bunker Hill was far from being decided. The outcome was hanging in the balance. Who would prevail?

The double scarlet-lines of foreign warriors proceeded forward. They were determined to capture the redoubt. The British ranks were much thinner than before. Again, it was a slow scarlet-advance against the rail fence. Again, it was a slow advance toward the breastwork and the redoubt. Again, the Americans waited until the British had scaled the last fence. Then Colonel Prescott gave the command. Fire! Just as before, the now familiar and devastating sound of thunderous American-musketry filled the Charlestown Peninsula. Bang! The first round of musketballs were fired followed by another and then another. Bang! Bang! Bang! All along the breastwork and all along the rail fence, American muskets were annihilating the Redcoats. As before, dozens of British officers were being maimed or killed. Scores and scores of rank-and-file Redcoats lay dead and wounded with their officers. Without any exaggeration, the entire hillside was covered with dead and dying Redcoats. The 5th and 52nd Regiments were being decimated by thousands of American musketballs fired in anger.

These young British-soldiers, who dreamt of returning to their island nation, were now dead. They were laying on two distant New England hills and a sorrowful beach far from home. The young lads from Essex and Kent, Northumberland and Cornwall, Sussex to the East Midlands and Wales; from the Scottish Highlands to the green rolling-hills of Ireland, the men from the cities of Edinburgh, Swansea, Manchester, Liverpool, London, Glasgow, Plymouth, Bristol, Dublin, Cardiff, Westminster and many more small towns and villages would dream no more of returning home. They had served their king and country well and could give no more. They were brave young-men. But now they were dead young-men laying upon the foreign soil of Charlestown, Massachusetts.

Incredibly General Howe continued to escape American musketballs. He just stood there in silent disbelieve viewing the massacre that encompassed him. The American patriots were proving that the grand British-strategy was indeed all wrong. It was dead wrong! General Howe had fearlessly and bravely led his men into battle, but he led many of them into the netherworld.

The British attack on their left resulted in General Pigot's division receiving a destructive firestorm of hot lead from the American redoubt. The British infantry, the 38th, 43rd and 47th Regiments and the First Royal Marines, couldn't get close enough to mount a bayonet charge. They were easily knocked down by American firepower. The Redcoats were falling by the dozens. It was a gruesome sight! The slaughter initiated their self-preservation mode. Men who survived their decimated ranks suddenly turned and ran. It was fight or flight! All along the British line, Redcoats scurried back to the bottom of the hill. They were trampling over their dead and wounded. It was a frightful demonstration of chaos and confusion. General Pigot's Redcoats unabashedly displayed a pathetic panic in their haste to escape the incessant stream of molten lead. Nobody could blame them for their actions on Breed's Hill. It was a macabre scene. The

British wounded were left to suffer where they fell. None of the British wounded were lent any support to escape from their personal hell. Only officers and especially high-ranking officers, such as the mortally wounded Lt. Colonel James Abercromby, would be offered some relief on the battlefield. Wounded Redcoats tried to get up and escape from the fighting. Few succeeded. Unable to escape the battlefield and with no help available; the wounded Redcoats once again fell down upon the hill and simply stayed there. Many of these wretched Redcoats bled for hours and would perish on these bloody New England-hills.

It has been estimated that the British light infantry and the Grenadiers had to survive approximately 30,000 musketballs during each of the first two-attacks. After the second attempt to storm the redoubt, the British lost nearly seventy-percent of their men. The light infantry company of the 35th Regiment was without a single officer or sergeant left standing. Some companies didn't even have a corporal to take charge and then the senior private became the man to follow.

The British were now losing the battle. They were losing badly! The unthinkable was happening! How could this be? The rebels were holding their ground. They were prevailing and winning! What went wrong with the British battle plan? Could this possibly be the end of the British fight? Would they have to board their little row-boats and return to Boston? Would they have to board their warships and evacuate Boston and there-fore all of Massachusetts and New England?

In his uncomplicated way, Colonel William Prescott tells us what hap-pened inside the redoubt:

"The enemy advanced and fired very hotly on the fort, and meeting with a warm reception, there was a very smart firing on both sides. After considerable time, finding our ammunition was almost spent, I com-manded a cessation till the enemy advanced within thirty-yards, when we gave them such a hot fire that they were obliged to retire nearly one-hun-dred and fifty-yards before they could rally."

Colonel Prescott's only son and noteworthy historian, Judge William Prescott, whose description of the Battle of Bunker Hill is looked upon as an excellent and fully reliable source, describes the American fire power inside the redoubt. Judge Prescott wrote the following:

"The discharge was simultaneous the whole length of the line, and though more destructive, as Colonel Prescott thought, than on the former assault, the enemy stood the first shock, and continued to advance and fire with great spirit; but before reaching the redoubt, the continuous, well directed fire of the Americans compelled them to give way, and they retreated for a second time, in greater disorder than before. Their officers were seen remonstrating, threatening, and even pricking and striking the soldiers, to urge them on, but in vain. Colonel Prescott spoke of it as a continued stream of fire from his whole line, from the first discharge to the retreat. The ground in front of the works was covered with the dead and wounded, some laying within a few yards." (28)

In Prescott's Redoubt and all along the American lines, loud euphoric-cheers could be heard. The cheers were so loud that perhaps they were heard all the way to Cambridge! These American patriots, who were wearing only home-spun-clothing, were defeating professional soldiers from the greatest army in the world. How could this be? The Americans were only militiamen at best. Yet the Americans were making a mockery of the professional army from Britain wearing their sharp looking professional uniforms. But clothing hardly mattered at the Battle of Bunker Hill. The fight in the soldier is what ultimately mattered. Both combatant armies had many courageous-warriors willing to fight to the death that calamitous day.

The Americans were momentarily reveling in their success. It was a boisterous celebration and perhaps premature. Plenty of danger still lurked nearby. General Howe was not finished with his mission. American gunpowder and ammunition were critically low. In fact, it was extremely low and all the patriots knew this to be true and so did the British! During the second attack, one of the patriots apparently was overheard saying very loudly that their ammunition was becoming quickly depleted. This glad tiding was quickly brought to the attention of General Howe. He was not ready to concede!

The Americans continued to be hungry, thirsty and scared. They were hoping that the British had enough of the battle and that maybe they had won the day. But that was just hope. The Redcoats regrouped once again.

Try, Try and Try Again for a Third Time

At the Charlestown Neck and extending into Cambridge, a scene of total disorganization was widespread in the American ranks. American reinforcements were afraid to cross the small strip of land into Charlestown. Some officers were simply not leading their men. In other instances, miscommunication totally ruled the moment for the Americans. Colonel

James Scammans, while marching his troops from Cambridge to Lechmere's Point, received a message from General Artemus Ward to go to the hill. The American fog of war suddenly appeared, because incredibly, Scammans interpreted this order as "go to Cobble Hill." That is exactly what he did. He took his troops to Cobble Hill. Cobble Hill was close enough to the Charlestown Neck, but was clearly the wrong hill to occupy. Cobble Hill is not on the Charlestown Peninsula.

Artillerist Major Scarborough Gridley, Engineer Colonel Richard Gridley's other officer-son, was currently at Cobble Hill shirking his duties. He had been ordered to go directly to Bunker Hill and enter the battle. Major Gridley decided to disobey his orders after witnessing a British cannonball bounding across the neck. Major Gridley had decided to stop at Cobble Hill instead. There he engaged in a useless fire-fight with *HMS Glasgow* and *HMS Symmetry.*

Meanwhile Captain Samuel Trevett who was under the command of Major Gridley ignored Gridley's orders to stop at Cobble Hill. Instead, Captain Trevett continued to proceed to the battle and the rail fence. Captain Trevett was towing his two cannons. Captain Trevett was simply disgusted with Major Gridley's cowardice. Shortly afterward, Colonel James Frye came along and asked Major Gridley what he was doing. Frye informed Gridley that his cannons were needed at the battle. Major Gridley balked at this order. Colonel Frye just sneered and scoffed at Major Gridley with disdain. Colonel Frye then left Cobble Hill and entered the battle after crossing the neck.

General Howe found himself once again at the bottom of Breed's Hill. It was now a familiar meeting-place for British troops to regroup. Perhaps he was pondering his costly mistakes. Maybe he was reflecting on the Province House meeting earlier in the morning when General Clinton suggested that British troops should surround the Charlestown Peninsula. None of this mattered now because it was too late in the day. Even if General Howe wanted to change course and land Redcoats by water behind the Americans; the ebb tide was to strong and wouldn't allow any British vessel to easily proceed down the river. Or perhaps, General Howe was possibly reflecting upon his own legacy. How would he, Major General William Howe, the pride of the British Army be remembered in the history books? He could only ponder about that. However, there were many more immediate and pressing problems for this commander to think about. His situation looked bleak. The fog of war was pleased.

General Howe called upon General Clinton to release the 63rd Regiment and the Second Royal Marines. With the peril of losing virtually every man in his army; General Howe decided he was going to risk a third attempt to take the redoubt and hopefully defeat these despicable Americans. Some of General Howe's officers begged him not to attack. It was prudent advice. General Howe ignored it. There were a few officers who agreed with General Howe's intention to attack once more. Afterall British honor was at stake. General Howe was a driven man and he was going to drive his men right up that infernal hill! He now had regained his composure and called upon his valor and honor. With this momentous decision to attack a third time, everything was on the line for General William Howe. It was now time to fight. Win or die!

General Clinton crossed over the Charles River from Copp's Hill. He proceeded to gather any walking wounded and all the stragglers which he could find. Together with General Pigot and the newly arrived 63rd Regiment and the Second Royal Marines, led by Major John Pitcairn; General Clinton would attempt to charge straight into the redoubt and "win the day" for the British. Both General Clinton and General Pigot were also driven men just like their commander and they too were expecting a British victory. They would have to fight hard and also hope for some luck.

General Howe observed that the one-hundred-yard gap between the breastwork and the rail fence was the American weak-link. This open area, along with the arrival of his reserves, plus the knowledge that the Americans were very low on ammunition had bolstered General Howe's courage to attack for a third time. He ordered his Redcoats to drop their heavy knapsacks and line up for a third assault. Would General William Howe prevail? Time would tell.

Assault of the Redoubt Once More

General Howe's short-term objective remained the same. It was the redoubt. As his Redcoats advanced upon the rail fence, he ordered his artillery forward. But this was just a feint. Eventually his artillerists successfully negotiated the sludgy ground and finally found a supportable position to fire at the breastwork. Further up the hill, Redcoats were stepping over the dead and wounded bodies of their countrymen and advancing toward the redoubt. Dozens of hapless British-wounded continued to writhe in pain and continued to suffer where they fell during the first two attacks. There were no medics or anybody to help them. General

Howe disregarded all of them. They had done their duty as good British soldiers.

As the British inched closer to the redoubt, General Howe suddenly turned his troops to the left. His Redcoats were now facing the breastwork and the redoubt all except his light infantry. British cannons continued to rake the breastwork and the three small-fleches with grapeshot from secured positions. This accurate bombardment chased the Americans from their positions. The Americans scattered into the redoubt or escaped to the rear toward Bunker Hill. A major link in the American defenses were now shattered. The light infantry continued firing at the rail fence with effective diversionary-fire. They were easily keeping Colonel Stark's men pinned down. When General Howe's main force swung to the left, they did so while firing a volley. The Redcoats in the rear ranks were now firing uphill at the fleeing Americans, but a lot of their musketballs were tragically sent into the backs of their countrymen. This did not stop the Redcoats. Gallantly and without any hesitation, the Redcoats pushed forward.

During this great disorder, some of the finest American-officers were killed or wounded while attempting to stop the collapse of their line. Colonel John Nixon and Colonel James Frye were wounded. Colonel Jonathan Brewer, Lt. Colonel William Buckminster, Adjutant Major John Butler were all killed. Major Willard Moore, who led Colonel Ephraim Doolittle's Regiment into battle, was also killed. Serving with Major Moore was Ensign Daniel Pike. He said Major Moore had been killed in the engagement. Ensign Pike was from Royalston, Massachusetts and survived the battle. Ensign Daniel Pike received a pension (Military Pension Fund S22441) and is the author's fourth-great-grandfather. He later settled in Waterford, Vermont. (29)

Inside Prescott's Redoubt virtually all the Americans had just three or four musketballs or even less to fire. Colonel Prescott remained confidant. He was that proverbial man who was solid as a rock. He was still encouraging his men to be steadfast and listen to his commands. The patriots inside the little fort had fought well. All throughout the battle, they had listened to Colonel Prescott's commands and were preparing to fire in unison with one last volley. Colonel Prescott had positioned the few men with bayonets in the likely areas where the enemy might attempt to gain entry into the little fort.

On top of Bunker Hill hundreds of men continued to be idle spectators. General Putnam was frustrated and exasperated. He was still trying to move men toward the fighting but to no avail. On the "safe side" or western side of Bunker Hill, General Putnam found Colonel Samuel Garrish laying on the ground. Garrish pleaded to General Putnam that he was completely exhausted. One of Gerrish's men said,

"The moment we came in sight of the enemy, "a tremor seiz'd" the fat colonel and "he began to bellow, Retreat! Retreat! Or you'll all be cut off! This so confused and scared our men that they retreated most precipitately." The only detachment from this outfit to see action was led by the gallant Dane, Adjutant Christian Febiger. He rallied a handful of men and took them into the fight at the rail fence. He later received accolades for his leadership. Febiger subsequently rose to the rank of colonel by 1779 in the Continental Army.

Men from Wethersfield, Connecticut arrived at the Charlestown Neck in time to witness the pandemonium. Captain John Chester said,

"When we arrived there was not a company with us in any kind of order, although, when we first set out, perhaps three regiments were by our side, and near us; but here they were scattered some behind rocks and hay-cocks, and 30 men, perhaps, behind an apple tree, frequently twenty men round a wounded man, retreating, when not more than three or four could touch him to advantage. Others were retreating, seemingly without any excuse, and some said they had left the fort with leave of the officers, because they had been all night and day on fatigue, without sleep, victuals, or drink; and some said they had no officers to lead them, which, indeed seemed to be the case."

Captain John Chester witnessed an entire company deserting that was led by their miscreant officers. He yelled at their commander and asked them why they were retreating. There was no answer. Captain Chester then gained the attention of the would-be deserters when he ordered his men to raise their guns. Captain Chester unhesitatingly threatened to shoot them unless they returned to the battle. These would-be deserters did an abrupt about-face and entered the fray once again.

On top of Bunker Hill Colonel Thomas Gardner's Regiment was met by General Putnam. "Old Put" immediately ordered one of Gardner's companies to work on his unfinished-fortification. Their effort was a futile endeavor. There simply was no time to build a proper fortification as the battle raged on. Sadly "Old Put" was totally fixated on the completion of his little fort. General Putnam's latest effort to finish his fortification wasn't benefiting the patriot cause in any way. Perhaps General Putnam should have exclusively focused himself on containing the advances of the oncoming British. But "Old Put" was headstrong and forceful. He was also losing any real control on top of Bunker Hill. It was too late into the battle to have entrenching tools put into the hands of warriors where firearms should have been held. The fog of war was now methodically operating on top of Bunker Hill. All of Colonel Gardner's men should have been sent at once to fight the British. Perhaps Colonel Gardner should have just ignored the orders from "Old Put" and proceeded to the battle. As we know, soldiers from a different colony were not legally obligated to follow orders from an officer of a different colony. But Colonel Gardner didn't demur or dispute General Putnam's orders. He clearly respected the general and put his men to work on behalf of General Putnam's fixation to build fortifications. If Colonel Gardner's men had immediately double-timed themselves straight to the redoubt, with their fresh supply of ammunition and powder, this would have undoubtedly bolstered the American cause. But, alas, this was not the reality of what happened to Colonel Gardner's Regiment. Despite the ongoing chaos and confusion, Colonel Gardner's regiment still played a crucial role toward the end of the battle.

One of the perturbing factors that American leaders struggled with; there were no reliable lines of communication between any of the commanding officers. Commanders had zero staff-officers to help coordinate any sort of battlefield-communication. Prior to the Battle of Bunker Hill, most likely the Americans didn't even discuss the possibility of clear lines of communication. The nature of eighteenth-century warfare presented particular-problems and real-time battlefield-communication was one of these pressing problems. The lack of insight and planning continued to hamper the American command, courtesy of the fog of war.

Directly behind the American redoubt, twenty-three-year-old Major Willard Moore was laying on the ground badly wounded. He had been carried to the redoubt from the breastwork. He was in dire need of water and suffering from the "death thirst." One of Moore's sergeants ordered his drummer boy to find something to drink for the major. The sergeant said to the youngster, "You are young and spry, so run to a pub and bring some rum or anything to drink, Major Moore is badly wounded. Go as quickly as possible." Robert Steele of Dedham, the youngest patriot in the redoubt was dispatched with this mission. He was joined by a boy from Boston named Benjamin Ballard. Benjamin knew the area well. They ran northward toward the neck. Benjamin knew where there was a tavern. Perhaps they would find refreshments there.

British cannonballs were whizzing overhead as the young patriots arrived at the pub. Only a short distance from them they witnessed perhaps as many as one-thousand Americans on the "safe side" of the neck. The Americans were completely reluctant to cross over into Charlestown. Now exhausted the youngsters entered the pub. They called out for the proprietor or anybody for help. There was no answer. Robert then stomped on the floor. A voice from the cellar asked them what they wanted. The boys said they were looking for some rum or water. The boys were instructed to take whatever they wanted. Robert took a two-quart earthen pitcher and filled it with rum. Benjamin filled a pail of water. To their credit, both of these brave young-patriots ventured to go where several-hundred would-be warriors wouldn't dare advance.

Meanwhile Captain John Chester led his men off Bunker Hill toward the front lines. One of his men, Samuel Webb said,

"Good God how the balls flew, I freely acknowledge I never had such a tremor. I confess, when I was descending into the Valley from off Bunker Hill, I had no more tho't of Ever rising the Hill again than I had of ascending to Heaven as Elijah did, Soul and Body together."

At the rail fence Colonel Stark's men were firing their muskets as fast as they could reload them. They were taking sharp aim at General Howe's light infantry and were also able to kill and wound some of the British artillerists further back on the battlefield. Colonel Stark's men were quickly depleting their ammunition. The New Hampshire frontier-marksmen and their New England brethren from Connecticut, were doing a superior job by effectively stymieing General Howe from flanking the redoubt. They were stopping the Redcoats from pouring into the redoubt from the rear. But their time was only ephemeral, as General Pigot's Redcoats were making progress on the south side of the redoubt.

The men from Massachusetts who were fighting in Charlestown, were eventually chased out of the smoldering ruins by the Redcoats. The Americans scampered to find any kind of shelter. They continued battling. They were hiding behind stone-walls, fences, rocks and a large-stone barn which was close to the redoubt. From these positions the Americans continued to dauntlessly harass the Redcoats. Major John Pitcairn and his Royal Marines were battling the Americans for every inch of ground on the slopes of Breed's Hill. The absence of any kind of patriot breastwork or flanking fortification on the south side of the redoubt was now very problematic for Colonel William Prescott. This was due to the courtesy of the fog of war.

Major General Dr. Joseph Warren's presence inside the redoubt was a steadying and calming effect for everybody. He was now fighting shoulder to shoulder with the men he loved. He talked to the men. He encouraged the men. Many words of comfort flowed from his heart and straight to his warriors.

Perhaps Major General Dr. Joseph Warren had a premonition that he wouldn't survive the battle. He had eluded to his possible death only a few days prior while talking to Dr. William Eustis. His loss would be a calamity for the American cause. His leadership was paramount to all the patriots of Massachusetts and throughout all the land which would eventually become the thirteen states of a new nation. When he spoke to the men his words were simple. He said,

"Hold steady boys. Listen to the colonel. Have a target. Make it count. We'll survive this. Hold steady. Hold steady boys."

Major General Dr. Joseph Warren was speaking to the men inside the redoubt when the two young-boys successfully returned with liquid refreshments. Their heroic effort temporarily helped to quench the thirst of the dying Major Willard Moore. The little that remained of the liquid refreshments didn't assuage or relieve all of the men inside the redoubt. Only a few lucky patriots had one sip of water or rum. It was really all for naught. Robert Steele later recalled, "It went very quick." Steele also alluded to finding some of the men in a confused state and talking about retreating.

Colonel Prescott was aware of the cowardly talk that was spreading in the redoubt. He was quick to make sure nobody deserted. The Americans were ferociously and successfully battling the British. Colonel Prescott wasn't going to let his men fall apart at this crucial moment. Colonel Prescott was determined not to lose the initiative and planned to continue the slap-down of the Redcoats once again. He needed every man to fight. He needed every man who ran from the breastwork to take his place at the redoubt firing-line. He needed any random patriot who valiantly made his way to the redoubt to take his place at the redoubt wall. Colonel Prescott was busy positioning his men where he needed them the most. He was once again preparing for battle, just as he had prepared all day long.

The incessant British heavy-bombardment ferociously continued.

Sergeant Benjamin Prescott the nephew of Colonel William Prescott, had previously been badly-wounded in the shoulder during the second attack. The young man was losing a lot of blood. He was subsequently ordered by Colonel Prescott to go to the rear of the redoubt and take care of himself as best that he could. When the fighting began again, Sergeant Prescott found a musket and attempted to enter the fight. When young Prescott was passing by the sally port, at the rear of the redoubt, an artillery shot hit Sergeant Prescott squarely smashing him into fragments.

Fight, Conquer Or Die

After the British cannons had finally vanquished the Americans at the three small-fleches and behind the breastwork; the 52nd Foot started mopping-up any stragglers coming from the fleches, while the 5th Foot and the Grenadiers mopped up at the breastwork. Meanwhile holding steady at the rail fence was Colonel Stark and his men. They were battling the British light infantry shot for shot. The main body of the Redcoats continued to push on. Their prize was right in front of them. The redoubt was close and American faces were starting to be discerned. The Battle of Bunker Hill was becoming even more personal than it already had been. Nothing but revenge now consumed the Redcoats. British bluster had energized the rank-and-file. British pride and honor drove the Redcoats forward. Their blind madness was carrying the day. "Fight, conquer, or die" became the incessant rallying call for the Redcoats. "Fight, conquer, or die!" (30)

The Redcoats were less than one-hundred yards away. "Fight, conquer, or die!" The battle cry of the enemy pervaded the air. Colonel Prescott continued to encourage his men. "Remember every shot must count. Don't fire unless you have a target."

The British appeared to be crazed! Perhaps they were. "Push on," they cried. "Fight, conquer, or die!" The enemy was now only fifty-yards away. Then forty-yards. The patriots showed great patience. They were listening intently for Colonel Prescott's command. They had participated in this act twice before. They knew what to do. The soot-laden faces of American patriots peered over the redoubt walls. Peter Brown took aim at the British; Major General Dr. Joseph Warren took aim, Amos Farnsworth took aim, and James Dodge, born in Edinburgh, Scotland took aim, Peter Salem took aim and all the patriots inside the redoubt took aim. The enemy was only thirty-yards away, then twenty-yards from the redoubt walls.

Colonel Prescott said with compelling confidence, "Fire!"

Bang! A tremendous concentrated-blaze shot out from American muskets. Bang! Bang! Bang! Once again and for a third time, British soldiers were collapsing on the hillside. American musketballs flew through the air into the intended targeted-Redcoats. American musketballs hit British foreheads and smashed through the arms and legs of the enemy. American musketballs flew into the chests and abdomens of many Redcoats, immediately destroying their bodies. The fierce American-volley successfully stopped the enemy in their place for a third time. The British reeled back. Defeat was looming for them. Some of the enemy Redcoats tried to stand up. They fell down again. There were countless Redcoats on the ground shrieking in pain all along their broken ranks. British officers were especially targeted. Officers were dying by the score! The American scythe was slicing the Redcoats to pieces. Foreign blood saturated the American soil in Charlestown. The Battle of Bunker Hill continued to be a frightful scene to behold. The British were being slaughtered once more!

On the southern slope of Breed's Hill, General Pigot's troops, the 47th Foot and the First Royal Marines pivoted around to the south side of the redoubt and slowly inched toward the fort. Major Pitcairn was leading the Royal Marines. His brave men followed closely behind him.

Bang! With the first American-volley fired at the Royal Marines, they too became casualties of Colonel Prescott's sharpshooting troops. The British fell back in confusion and in similar fashion as General Howe's men did only moments ago. Dozens of Redcoats fell dead or wounded. The Redcoats were dazed but they remained resilient. If necessary, these good English-soldiers would die as Englishmen on this sorrowful and dreadful faraway-hill. Dozens of Welsh, Scottish and Irish soldiers would also sacrifice their lives and die on this bloody hill.

The outcome of the Battle of Bunker Hill still remained uncertain.

The Royal Marines were now firing at the redoubt but they had orders to exclusively make a bayonet charge. Some of the military-tactics of the British were rather strange. Why would British warriors be ordered not to fire their muskets during battle? The British definitely had their own unique ideas of how an army should function and fight during combat.

Almost immediately after the first volley; Adjutant John Waller was doing his best to gather up the Redcoats trying to keep them in formation. Waller also attempted to stop the Redcoats from firing their muskets. The American patriots were watching Waller, as he scurried about in near panic. Waller's frenzied activity must have been puzzling to the Americans.

Meanwhile Major Pitcairn had mistakenly thought the Americans had abandoned the redoubt. He shouted to his men that the rebels were gone. Enter the fog of war. Pitcairn then heard somebody in the redoubt proclaim that, "We are not all gone." The voice that he heard was the patriot who was about to shoot the popular major dead. Peter Salem raised his freedom musket and aimed at the British Redcoat. Salem pulled the trigger. Bang! Major John Pitcairn fell mortally wounded! He grasped at his chest and fell into his son's arms. Pitcairn told his son William to go back to his men. But William accompanied his father to Boston. He died there soon afterward. Major Pitcairn was buried at the Old North Church in Boston. Pitcairn was replaced on the bloody hill by gallant Adjutant John Waller.

The courageous Redcoats managed to surge forward. Inside the redoubt patriot defenders were quickly depleting the last of their ammunition and gunpowder. They were still listening for the commands of Colonel Prescott. Over the course of several hours, they had quickly become disciplined warriors. But the moment was dire. There wouldn't be another simultaneous thunderous-shot coming from Prescott's Redoubt. American fire-power was finally fizzling out! The fog of war was thriving!

The Redcoats continued to press on. The British were determined to "win the day" or die fighting for the crown. The patriot defenders now were firing their last one or two musketballs. After each American had expended the last of his ammunition; rocks, random nails or just about any object that could possibly become a projectile, was rammed down the barrels of patriot muskets. As long as there was any gunpowder remaining, the Americans would attempt to fire something or anything at the oncoming enemy. It was truly a brave but pitiful sight to behold. And the fog of war didn't miss a beat.

Some of the Americans inside Colonel Prescott's little fort were making personal vows to themselves, their friends and to the men fighting beside them. They vowed not to abandon the redoubt. They vowed to fight till the last man was standing. The legendary Battle of Bunker Hill had yet to be decided!

Close to the redoubt, glistening fourteen-inch bayonets were pointed toward the little fort by deranged Redcoats. They were only focused on vengeance. They had become wrathful men. They had just witnessed the deaths of hundreds of their own countrymen suffering terribly in the last moments of their lives. The Redcoats were struck down by these loath-some rebels hiding behind the earthen walls of the redoubt. The Redcoats dearly wanted and emotionally needed to extract major revenge on these vulgar yokels of New England. For these British soldiers, there wasn't any time to think about anything else. There was only time to charge the re-doubt. "Fight, conquer, or die."

The Scarlet Storm Has Arrived

Through sheer determination and courage, the British charged forward and finally made their way into a ditch that surrounded the redoubt. Captain George Harris and Lt. Francis Rawdon led the way. Some of the Grenadiers followed closely behind them. The Redcoats kept as close to the outside walls of the little fort as best that they could. Closer was definitely safer. From this position, they would attempt to scale the wall and charge into the redoubt. Harris made the first attempt to gain entry into Prescott's Redoubt. He was repelled. The American defenders clubbed his legs with their muskets. A second time he was driven back. On his last attempt a musketball grazed the top of his head. He fell into Rawdon's arms and was whisked away by four Grenadiers. Redcoats carried him to their small boats moored in Boston Harbor for evacuation.

Shortly afterward, the badly wounded Major Arthur Williams made his way into the ditch and was twisting in agony. Rawdon ordered Ensign Martin Hunter to find some medical help. But there wasn't any help to be found. Ensign Hunter realized he was much safer exactly where he was. He was tight up against the wall of the redoubt. If Hunter had attempted to carry out Rawdon's order, this would have been his death warrant and he knew it. He disobeyed his order. Hunter balked at leaving and later said,

"Though a very young soldier, I had sense enough to know that I was much safer close under the works than I could be at a few yards from it, as the enemy could not depress their arms sufficiently to do any execution to those that were close under, and to have gone to the rear to look for a surgeon would have been almost certain death; indeed, the Major was not a very great favorite with me as he had obliged me to sell a pony that I had bought for seven and sixpence."

Even for eighteenth-century standards, it remains peculiar that military leaders lacked the insight to supply battlefield medics for their combat troops. The fact that Ensign Hunter would have to travel an insufferable distance to find medical help was unacceptable to him. Hunter should have merely been able to yell for a medic, but that would be too logical and easy. The ever-troublesome fog of war was again making another inopportune appearance and this time it was harassing the British.

General Howe and his officers were sending as many men as they could across the ditch to support Lt. Francis Rawdon and his small group of Redcoats. They were waiting for more reinforcements to eventually storm the redoubt. Lt. Rawdon and his Redcoats stayed closely huddled up against the wall of the redoubt.

Finally General Howe was wounded. He received a musketball in his foot. It was his turn to suffer. The British commander amazingly had escaped patriot gunfire until now. General Howe's wound was far from life threatening. His aide Major John Small rushed to help General Howe even though Small had a musketball lodged in his own shoulder.

A patriot sniper whose name has also been lost to the pages of history, was courageously firing muskets at a quickened pace. He would fire his round, then hand off his musket to a fellow patriot who in return passed him another loaded musket. In the last few minutes of this American hero's life, a British soldier estimated that he killed no less than 20 officers. Consequently, he became an urgent target for the Redcoats. He was signaled out by the crazed Redcoats. He was shot dead by a charging Redcoat sergeant. This patriot portrayed American selflessness and courage of the highest order. He represented everything that fighting for freedom meant to the Americans at the Battle of Bunker Hill.

Abruptly Prescott's Redoubt went silent from any patriot blast. Royal Marine Adjutant John Waller said later,

"Suddenly their flame went out like a spent candle."

Immediately access to the redoubt became much easier for the British. Colonel Prescott ordered his men to manhandle the muskets out of the hands of the Redcoats and to use their own muskets as clubs. One British officer, Lt. Richardson of the Royal Irish climbed to the top of the parapet and proclaimed,

"The day is ours!" (31)

He was bayoneted and shot by Captain Ebenezer Bancroft. He fell back over the parapet. Several more of Lt. Richardson's countrymen were now on top of the parapet. They too were shot down by some of the patriots in the back of the redoubt. Each of these patriots had one last musketball to fire and they used it well.

Shortly after Adjutant John Waller had regained sufficient order of his men, the British leapt over the ditch and climbed the parapet. The Redcoats stormed the redoubt, while continuing to step over their dead and dying brothers. Waller and the Royal Marines and the men from the 52nd Regiment were some of the first British-warriors to enter the redoubt. Still undaunted the Americans fought ferociously. They fought as equally crazed as the foreign invaders. Savage and brutal fighting took place over the course of several minutes inside the redoubt.

In a letter dated June 22, 1775, a newspaper states that young Lt. Richardson of the Royal Irish was the first to mount the parapet. First Lt. John Clark's narrative stated that the remains of a company of the 63rd Regiment of Grenadiers were the first Redcoats that succeeded in entering the redoubt. After Captain Horsford had been wounded and Lt. Dalrymple had been killed, a sergeant took command and beseeched the Redcoats, saying,

"We must either conquer or die." (32)

The British then entered the works. General Gage later recommended the brave sergeant for promotion.

Up and over the berm of the redoubt came more Redcoats. It was similar to an inundation bursting forth from a dam. They were flooding into the little fort. The Americans were flailing at the enemy with whatever they could use. They were using their muskets as clubs in the attempt to stem the oncoming red-tide. The defenders were picking up rocks and random pieces of wood to smash the surging enemy. Then vicious hand to hand combat began. The Americans were using their strength and strong will to remain alive. The British were using their strength and strong will to prevail.

Colonel Prescott was skillfully parrying his sword in an attempt to stop the trusts of Redcoats wielding their fourteen-inch bayonets. It was mayhem inside the little fort! The dust was chokingly thick. Dirt was kicked up all around the redoubt. Americans were being mauled by the British long-blades. The patriots who vowed to fight on till the end were becoming casualties. Many Americans died at the hands of British bayonets in these last few minutes. One British officer claimed that as many as 30 Americans were killed by British bayonets inside the redoubt. Dozens of Americans were laying dead everywhere inside their little fort. Another British officer declared that the Americans fought more like devils than men.

Judge Prescott writes:

"The British had entered the redoubt, and were advancing, when Colonel Prescott ordered a retreat. He was among the last; and before leaving it, was surrounded by the enemy, who had entered, and had several passes with the bayonet made at his body, which he parried with his sword, of use of which he had some knowledge." (33)

After Colonel Prescott had ordered a retreat, some of his men jumped over the redoubt walls only to find themselves in the midst of the oncoming Redcoats. Young Peter Brown was one of these men. He said in a letter to his mother, "I ran a half mile while balls flew like hailstones and cannon roared like thunder."

Brown continued, "If we should be called to action again, I hope to have the courage and strength to act my part valiantly in defence of our liberty and country, trusting in Him who hath yet kept me, and hath covered my head in the day of battle; and though we have left four out of our company, and some taken captives by the cruel enemies of America, I was not suffered to be touched, although I was in the fort when the enemy came in, and jumped over the walls." (34)

The redoubt was quickly surrounded on three sides. The small sally port at the rear of the redoubt was becoming clogged with men. There was a rush to get out but not a full-fledged panic. A heavy layer of smoke and dust hung inside the fort and this hindered the progress of most of the retreating men. They were hurriedly guiding themselves to the exit by feeling the walls. Once outside Colonel Prescott was urging his men to run quickly but separately and not bunch together. He continued to masterfully parry bayonet thrusts coming toward him. He was one of the last patriots to retreat out of the redoubt.

Major General Dr. Joseph Warren was also one of the last men to leave the redoubt. Before he left the little fort, Dr. Joseph Warren and an unknown number of patriots fought furiously to keep the sally port open for the last patriots to exit. Because of this group of brave men, more Americans successfully were able to escape out of the doomed fort and survive. The redoubt had now become a death trap for the Americans. After exiting the redoubt, the Americans hastily ran for safety. They ran for their lives!

When Colonel Prescott, Major General Dr. Joseph Warren and the remaining American troops were exiting the redoubt; Colonel Stark, Captain Knowlton and some of Colonel Gardner's troops, which included the Charlestown company, left their position at the rail fence and executed a very effective flanking-maneuver. This action helped to quell the hard charging Redcoats. The men from the rail fence were also firing the last of their ammunition and gunpowder. Additionally, effective firing-cover from Captain Seth Washburn and his men had securely covered everybody leaving the rail fence.

Captain Ebenezer Bancroft was one of the last to get out of the redoubt. He had lost his treasured old French-gun to a Redcoat who had pilfered it from his hands. In turn, Bancroft then ripped a musket out of the hands of another Redcoat and killed him with its bayonet. Immediately Captain Bancroft lost this musket too! He jumped over the wall of the redoubt only to find a Redcoat standing right next to him. Bancroft started to run for his life, but then he stopped. He realized that the Redcoat would certainly shoot him in the back. So, Bancroft turned around and smashed the Redcoat in the face. The British soldier was dazed by the unexpected punch. The stunned Redcoat fell back and hit the ground. Captain Bancroft started running. He was badly wounded but he managed to escape and survive. He lost the forefinger on his left hand, had his shoulder smashed in and was sightless in one eye. He ran to the safety of Bunker Hill and made his way across the neck and back to Cambridge.

Another patriot who fought the Redcoats inside the redoubt and survived was Amos Farnsworth. When he exited the redoubt, he was wounded with a musketball in his right arm. He said,

"I received a wound in my rite arm, the bawl gowing through a little below my elbow breaking the little shel bone. Another bawl struck my back, taking a piece of skin about as big as a penny. But I got to Cambridge that night."

It's Time to Retreat

Not long after Colonel Prescott ordered a retreat, there were significantly more British inside the redoubt than Americans. Due to the lack of gunpowder and musketballs, Colonel Prescott's little redoubt had finally fallen to the British enemy!

To the credit of the British Army, they had fought courageously and superbly. They had conquered the redoubt; however, a multitude of British soldiers had died while doing so. The Redcoats persevered and kept true to their rallying cry of, "Fight, conquer or die!" Although the British gained the redoubt, they paid a high-price to bellow out their war cry at the little American-fort.

The fighting in and around the redoubt raged on for five or six more dreadful minutes. Stand and fight was still on the minds of some of the patriots, including Major General Dr. Joseph Warren and Colonel William Prescott. Both of these American leaders had vowed not to be taken alive. Both men were now out of the redoubt and were calmly walking toward Bunker Hill. The Redcoats made a halfhearted attempt to chase the patriots to Bunker Hill, but they were ordered not to pursue them very far.

During the American retreat, British grapeshot was unremitting and working well. The British were exacting a heavy toll on the fleeing patriots. There were now as many as one-thousand Americans gathered at the top of Bunker Hill. The Americans were not going anywhere except down the backside of Bunker Hill and then off the peninsula to safety. They were retreating to the mainland as fast as they could go. Meanwhile General William Howe was demonstrating some prudence by not pursuing them. He didn't know the American intentions and wisely held back his troops. He didn't want to risk being attacked. General Howe didn't want to blindly pursue the rebels and thereby prolong this hellish battle.

General Howe was wounded, battered, blood-soaked and to some extent bewildered and shocked. How could he not be bewildered and shocked? All he had to do was take a look around and view what he and General Thomas Gage had unleashed. All of his aides were either killed or wounded. His army had been cut to ribbons. In some of his companies there were only three, four or five men left standing. Officers by the score were dead, dying or wounded. General Howe had enough of this battlefield disaster. His troops were decimated by the men that he didn't believe would stand and fight. Perhaps now the general understood the American fighting man much better. The fog of war was all around General Howe, three-hundred and sixty-degrees. This renown military-tactician was forced to grasp the limits of his army and perhaps himself. The whole affair was a catastrophe. General William Howe's troops gained the redoubt, but what did he gain?

Meanwhile on top of Bunker Hill, General Israel Putnam was surrounded by troops who still had zero inclination to get involved in the fighting. He had little to no control over most of them. General Putnam had realized too late into the battle that the redoubt was clearing out. British grapeshot was now raking the fleeing patriots. General Putnam then spurred his horse down the eastern side of the hill. General Putnam abruptly turned around because British artillery-fire was too fierce. He quickly rode back up the hill.

One Massachusetts colonel who did heed Putnam's call was Colonel Gardner. General Putnam ordered Colonel Gardner and the remainder of his split regiment to double-time their pace toward the redoubt. This is when Colonel Gardner was shot in the groin and was mortally wounded. His son ran over to help him. Colonel Gardner ordered him back into the fight. The fog of war wasn't leaving the Americans or the fight any time soon.

It was during this frantic time, that practically all the Americans who were on top of Bunker Hill started to retreat. They were making their way down Bunker Hill toward the Charlestown Neck as fast as they could go. British gondolas and ships, close enough to the neck, were firing as rapidly as they could at the retreating men. The British stood unopposed. The Americans had no way to counter this floating misery. The fleeing Americans were being raked with grapeshot and cannon-shot. It was truly a chaotic scene. Americans casualties quickly mounted as they descended off Bunker Hill.

By now dozens of Americans had been killed fleeing the enemy. Many patriots fell on their native soil that connected Breed's Hill to Bunker Hill. Meanwhile, Major John Brooks had finally been released by General Artemus Ward. He was leading two companies when he arrived at the neck. Major Brooks missed the battle but he witnessed the chaos. He futilely attempted to organize the men as they walked by him.

Major John Brooks sadly said, "The brow of Bunker Hill was the place of great slaughter."

Major General Dr. Joseph Warren was courageous and stubborn. He didn't want to give up the fight. General Dr. Joseph Warren tried to rally several men as they were retreating but they were leaving as fast as they could. When Dr. Joseph Warren turned around to survey the situation, a large volley was fired by several Redcoats. A musketball hit Dr. Joseph Warren in the head. He died instantly. The British later buried him approximately where he fell. He shared a shallow grave with another American hero. When General Dr. Joseph Warren's body was finally exhumed, he was identified by Paul Revere. Revere identified his own dental work which he had provided to General Dr. Joseph Warren.

After the Battle of Bunker Hill, General Johnny Burgoyne made these complimentary comments regarding the American retreat.

"It was no flight: it was covered with bravery and military skill."

Lt. Rawdon, who survived the vicious fight up the hill and inside the redoubt praised the Americans. Lt. Rawdon said,

"The Americans put up a running fight; one fence, or wall, to another."

To the credit of the New England Army every effort was made to rescue their wounded. The American wounded were carried to the western side of Bunker Hill and then to Cambridge. Some of the wounded went to the Vassall mansion or sent to the houses of former Lt. Governor Andrew Oliver and Reverend Samuel Cook. These homes became hospitals. The wounded were treated by Doctors Thomas Kittredge, William Eustis, Walter Hastings, Thomas Welsh, Isaac Foster, David Townsend, John Hart and Lt. Colonel Dr. James Brickett. As the reader will recall, Lt. Colonel Dr. James Brickett was wounded at the battle but continued his outstanding service to the American cause. The wounded Americans who died in Cambridge were buried in a field in front of the Oliver house.

The British still managed to take 30 Americans as prisoners of war. Regrettably for many of the Americans, they were badly wounded and couldn't be rescued by the end of the battle. Timothy Kettle, age unknown, was a young lad from Charlestown and was held among the prisoners. The British listed him as dismissed and not counted as a prisoner of war. Twenty men died in captivity. (35)

After running major-interference and protecting the patriots coming out of the redoubt; the warriors from the rail fence retreated back to the neck by the northern road. This road ran over the summit of Bunker Hill. Most of Colonel Prescott's men coming out of the redoubt had retreated on the southern road. This road ran close to the base of Bunker Hill continuing near the Mill Pond and on toward the neck.

General Putnam still maintained the hope of making a stand on Bunker Hill. His little fort remained quite unfinished. At the end of the battle, all of General Putnam's efforts to build fortifications on top of Bunker Hill amounted to an exercise of futility. General Putnam tried in vain to rally the patriot troops one last time. It was to no avail. General Putnam was ignored. It was a hopeless scene on top of Bunker Hill. Escape and survival was the only concern for the rank-and-file Americans. General Putnam finally realized that the end of the battle for the Charlestown Peninsula had arrived. He eventually made his way down from Bunker Hill and crossed over to the mainland. Within one-hour, General Putnam was fortifying both Prospect Hill and Winter Hill. This high ground was not far from the Charlestown Neck. If the British crossed over the Charlestown Neck; General Putnam was preparing to be ready to meet this formidable enemy once again.

The Connecticut militiamen immediately started to build new fortifications. Prospect Hill and Winter Hill are directly opposite the Charlestown Neck. Prospect Hill is 95 feet-high. Winter Hill is only 43 feet-high. This elevated ground was a good location for a military stronghold. "Old Put" had managed to salvage some of the entrenching tools and carried them to these positions. The old American warrior just seemed tireless.

Lt. Experience Storrs wrote, "We immediately went to entrenching; flung up by morning an entrenchment one-hundred feet square. Done principally by our regiment under Putnam's directions, had but little sleep that night."

Approaching the Charlestown Neck, the retreating Americans started to converge upon each other. A bottleneck was forming. This began the gridlock of men crossing the small isthmus. Near panic set in when cannonading from *HMS Glasgow* and *HMS Symmetry* raked the neck. At its narrowest width, the Charlestown Neck was a little over one-hundred feet wide. Approximately one-thousand Americans were attempting to flee to the mainland. Men were being torn apart by British cannon-fire. Any orderly retreat was gone. Chaos reigned for minutes. Men pushed and they shoved carelessly trampling over the wounded. The last of their energy was spent trying to rush across the causeway. It was a pathetic and ugly scene. The Americans were totally helpless. Dozens of men fell from the cannon fire. The fog of war pursued the Americans right off the peninsula.

General Clinton eventually found General Howe in the middle of the battlefield. General Howe was standing in the midst of the debacle which he created. Upon first glance, perhaps there was a moment of "I told you so." Perhaps not. One thing was certain, there was enough shock to go around for every rank-and-file Redcoat, not just the generals or other high ranking-officers. Attempting to come to terms with this massive British failure would assuredly take some time for these haughty British-generals. General Clinton still had a fight in him. He tried to convince General Howe to let him pursue the Americans all the way to Cambridge. General Clinton still had fresh troops with the Second Royal Marines and the 63rd Regiment. But the answer was no. It was a prudent answer. Vaunted General William Howe was spent.

General Clinton then ordered his troops to secure Captain John Montresor's small fortification on top of Bunker Hill. It faced west and looked down at the Charlestown Neck. Engineer Montresor had built this small fortification when the British retreated to Bunker Hill on April 19, 1775.

It was now past the five o'clock hour. The battle was over. Situated just west of the neck were Americans inside several houses. They were keeping close watch on the Redcoats. Sporadic firing could still be heard. The Americans inside the houses were close enough to Charlestown that occasioned them to take potshots at the Regulars. The Redcoats returned their fire. Eventually, all the guns fell silent.

Major Andrew McClary who had survived the Battle of Bunker Hill had retreated back to Medford. After talking to Captain Henry Dearborn they decided that it would be beneficial to go back to the Charlestown Neck and scout the area. They had no orders to do so. McClary wanted to see if the British were assembling for the purpose of crossing the neck to march toward Cambridge. McClary daringly crossed the neck to reconnoiter the enemy. Satisfied that the British were not mobilizing he started back to his command. A British sailor saw him from the vantage point of his warship. One of the last cannon-shots of the Battle of Bunker Hill was fired by *HMS Glasgow*. It smashed Major McClary to bits. He may have been the last American to die at the Battle of Bunker Hill on June 17, 1775. We will never know for sure if Captain McClary was the last patriot to die at the Battle of Bunker Hill. Why? Because approximately around this same time; two Americans who were hiding in one of the unburned houses of Charlestown came out of the house and casually strolled up to a British company led by Lt. John Dutton. Dutton believed that the Americans were simply going to surrender. The Americans proceeded to shoot and kill Dutton and his orderly. The Americans in turn were chased down and bayoneted to death by Dutton's men.

After escaping from the battle, while utterly exhausted and frazzled to their bones, the American warriors welcomed their current relief from cannon fire, musketballs and half-mad wrathful-Redcoats determined to run them through with their bayonets. They urgently needed something to eat and drink. They slogged along hardly uttering a word. They arrived at the American camps in Cambridge or Medford and finally found some relief.

Battle Aftermath

The grim reality of British casualties now permeated the town of Boston. The healthy surviving-Redcoats had the grisly task of locating their dead and wounded countrymen still laying on the hills of Charlestown. Countless dozens of men were suffering terribly. Some of the Redcoats had been on the ground bleeding for hours. These wounded Redcoats were taken to the shore and transported to Boston. Some of the wounded managed to survive. Dead Redcoats were buried on the hills. American patriots were also buried by the British on these infernal bloody-hills. It was a gruesome sight. It was a gruesome task to bury so many men.

Every available boat in Boston, whether small or large, made several trips across Boston Harbor to ferry the Redcoats from Charlestown to their barracks. Makeshift hospitals were situated throughout the town. Some of the British wounded went home. Shocked soldiers wandered about the streets. There was widespread disbelief by everybody in Boston. How did this happen? Squalls of anguish and grief rang out from family members of the Regulars who were killed.

The British suffered 226 killed and 828 wounded, for a staggering count of 1,054 men. There were 92 officers killed or wounded. The American tactic of targeting British officers clearly succeeded.

Nobody said it better than General Henry Clinton, when he succinctly summed up the disastrous British experience, when he wrote, "A dear bought victory, another such would have ruined us." (36)

Was the Battle of Bunker Hill a victory for the British? Perhaps not.

General Thomas Gage in a letter to Lord Barrington said,

"My Lord, you will receive an account of some success against the Rebels, but attended with a long list of killed and wounded, so many of the latter that the hospital hardly has hands sufficient to take care of them... These people shew a Spirit and Conduct against us they never shewed against the French, and everybody has Judged of them from their former appearance and behavior when joined with the Kings Forces in the last War; which has led many into great mistakes. They are now spirited up by Rage and Enthusiasm, as great as ever People were possessed of, and you must proceed in earnest or give the Business up. You must have large armies making diversions on different sides, to divide their force. The loss we have Sustained is greater than we can bear. Small Armies can't afford such losses especially when the advantage gained tends to little more than the gaining of a post-a material one indeed as our own security depends on it. The troops are sent out to late, the rebels were at least two months before-hand with us and your Lordship would be astonished to see the tract of country they have entrenched and fortified; their number is great, so many have been employed…I have before written your Lordship my opinion that a large army must at length be employed to reduce these people and mentioned the hiring of foreign troops. I fear it must come to that or else to avoid a land war and make use only of your fleet."

General Gage continued, "I wish this Cursed Place was burned!"

To his credit, General William Howe was able to praise both General Clinton and General Pigot for their leadership and resolute belief that the British would "win the day." If not for the steadfast leadership of both General Clinton and General Pigot, perhaps General Howe's third assault on the redoubt would have failed regardless of the plight of low ammunition and no gunpowder suffered by the Americans. General Howe was rightfully giving credit to those who deserved it. In thoughtful retrospection; maybe General Howe recalled how he and General Thomas Gage quickly dismissed General Clinton's plans as unworthy at the meeting held at Province House. Now perchance, both generals would learn to respect this annoying and often insufferable man. Ironically almost three years later, General Clinton would replace General Howe, as the British Commander in Chief of all British forces in the American Revolutionary War.

After the Battle of Bunker Hill and the wanton destruction of Charlestown; American patriots everywhere viewed the British as barbaric savages. Reconciliation was long gone and now quite impossible. The progression of violence starting years earlier, with the terrible Boston Massacre, had reached its zenith with the Battle of Bunker Hill.

Within hours of the Battle of Bunker Hill, both Colonel Prescott and General Clinton wanted to resume the fight. Colonel Prescott was adamant about retaking the Charlestown Peninsula. He requested one-thousand men to march as soon as possible. General Clinton still wanted to march on to Cambridge. The folly of each request was masquerading as everybody's familiar nemesis, the fog of war.

General Artemus Ward immediately denied Colonel Prescott's request. Colonel Prescott was angry from the lack of support afforded him. Colonel Prescott later lamented that if his men only had more ammunition and gunpowder, he was certain they would have "carried-the-day" and would have held the redoubt. Most likely Colonel Prescott would have prevailed.

The Americans were now in worse shape than prior to the Battle of Bunker Hill. The patriots assuredly had less ammunition and gunpowder than before the battle. The little army of New England was also in its familiar state of flux and organizational inadequacy. This wasn't a new set of circumstances for the Americans. This nascent New England Army had been struggling with disorganization since the first patriot-warriors arrived in Cambridge in April. The Americans were still experiencing the fog of war and its aftermath of uncertainty.

On Sunday the day after the battle, General Gage held a meeting with his generals. They hotly discussed and argued their predicament and suggested future plans. General Gage was now finally coming to terms with the British reality in Massachusetts. He said it was pointless to try to hold onto Boston. General Howe believed that holding Boston was all that the British could possibly do. With his usual dose of bravado, rash General Clinton proposed another offensive. This time he wanted to assault the Americans by going through Dorchester. Amazingly this time General Gage agreed with him. An assault was planned for the following Saturday. Would the British be ready for battle in one week? Would General Gage be foolish enough to send his depleted troops to meet the Americans once again?

On Saturday the Redcoats were already in their light boats when the operation was suddenly called off. Why did General Gage renege on this attack especially at the very last moment? We may never know exactly why. General Gage had all week to think about this pending attack. He simply called off the operation. Most likely General Gage didn't want a possible repeat of Bunker Hill so soon after the disastrous battle. It took him until the last moments of the pending attack to realize the folly of it all. This wouldn't be the last time the British would entertain the idea of securing Dorchester Heights and break out of Boston. After the recall of General Gage, General Howe would have his own chance to break out of Boston in less than a year.

The British continued to suffer for many months and reinforcements were never sent by the British government.

The Siege of Boston continued.

Several weeks after the carnage of the Battle of Bunker Hill the American camp witnessed big changes. Supplies started to arrive in Cambridge from every part of the country. Previous fortifications which ran from Chelsea to the Boston Neck were strengthened tremendously. Any lines of communication, which may have existed with the British, were now long gone. Both camps were taciturn toward the other. At the American camp in Cambridge; men still left for home while others arrived to take their place and commerce still prevailed among some of the more enterprising militiamen.

One new arrival in the American camp was a tall Virginian named George Washington. Only a few weeks earlier, General George Washington had been appointed commander of all American forces by the Second Continental Congress. He rode into Cambridge on July 3, 1775, escorted by Moses Gill. Gill was the Chairman of the Committee of Supplies and would later become Acting Governor of Massachusetts in 1799. General George Washington took command of the New England Army from the gracious and steadfast General Artemus Ward. He immediately worked on improving the morale and the military readiness of the American patriots. General George Washington's little army eventually became the core of the Continental Army.

One year and one day later, the Declaration of Independence was signed, on July 4, 1776, in Philadelphia.

A new nation of Americans rejoiced!

Part Three: The Aftermath

Who Won the Battle of Bunker Hill?

Who won the Battle of Bunker Hill? Should historians consider the British possession of the Charlestown Peninsula a victory? Or does the massive amount of British casualties suffered at Bunker Hill embody a defeat? The Americans were able to stop the Redcoats from advancing any further than Charlestown. Does this exemplify an American victory? Yet the Americans were driven from the Charlestown Peninsula. Does this symbolize an American defeat? Did the outcome of the Battle of Bunker Hill benefit the British more or the Americans more?

In the immediate aftermath of the battle and many decades into the future, Americans looked upon the Battle of Bunker Hill as a loss. Even today, nearly two and one-half centuries later, it is common to read that the British won the battle. Yes, the British gained the redoubt and forced the Americans out of the peninsula. They deservedly shouted, "The Day is Ours" after their amazing display of perseverance and limitless-courage. But it was a hollow shout. In the eighteenth-century one of the parameters of a military victory was gaining the ground of enemy territory just as it still may be today. An army simply fought and drove the enemy out of its position to "win the day." The British achieved this objective by ejecting the Americans from the strategic hills of Charlestown with an enormous amount of help from the fog of war. However, Charlestown is where the British were stopped. They advanced no further. Their ultimate goal had eluded them. The British didn't come close to capturing Cambridge or any other territory of the new State of Massachusetts. The British willingly paid an enormous price in blood for Charlestown. Their casualties were staggering. General Gage's major mistake of withdrawing all his troops off the Charlestown Peninsula on April 20, 1775, was precarious. The Battle of Bunker Hill was the steep price that he paid for his monumental calamity. Finally, General Gage failed in his attempt to apprehend any of the American military or civilian-leadership.

The Battle of Bunker Hill has been described as a "pyrrhic victory" and perhaps tantamount to a British defeat. One British officer suggested this opinion of the battle, when he said,

"Too great a confidence in ourselves which is always dangerous occasioned this dreadful loss." We are all wrong at the head. My mind cannot help dwelling upon our cursed mistakes. Such ill conduct at the first outset argues a gross ignorance of the most common rules of the profession and gives us for the future anxious forebodings, I have lost some of those I most valued. The brave men's lives were wantonly thrown away. Our conductor [General William Howe] as much murdered them as if he had cut their throats himself on Boston Common. Had he fallen; ought we have regretted him?"

The aforementioned account, of the conduct of battlefield-commander General William Howe, is the most scathing written opinion that any British soldier offered regarding General Howe's leadership at the Battle of Bunker Hill.

The poignant memories of Bunker Hill would go on to haunt the British for the remainder of the American Revolutionary War. Often during the eight-years of the conflict, the British simply were reluctant to pursue the Americans with any great-sense of urgency. Perhaps their hesitation was the result of the massive amount of casualties taken on the hills of Charlestown.

During the remainder of General Howe's command in the American Revolutionary War, he always remembered the lessons that he learned while attacking Prescott's Redoubt. Subsequently he became adverse to ordering his men into a frontal attack.

The New England militiamen with their drab-brown homespun-clothing stood up and fought the powerful and vaunted army of Great Britain. The Americans fought with determination and courage. The casualties that they inflicted upon the British were breathtaking. The British didn't see this coming. The Redcoats suffered terribly at the Battle of Bunker Hill. This was due in part because of the disdain and arrogance promoted by General Thomas Gage and General William Howe toward the American fighting men. The Battle of Bunker Hill wasn't a primrose path for the British. It was a treacherous path that led to a wretched conclusion.

Again, who won the Battle of Bunker Hill? For the British, perhaps at best it was a draw. The British gained little territory for a disproportionate amount of dead and wounded. The British finally lost the Siege of Boston and were driven from the free and independent state of Massachusetts nine-months after the Battle of Bunker Hill. For the Americans; the punishment delivered to the British and the subsequent psychological-paralysis inflicted upon them benefitted the Americans throughout the whole length of the war. At the end of the legendary day of June 17, 1775, the Americans were still intact and would soon be ready to fight once again. The preceding reasons are why the author argues that the Americans won the Battle of Bunker Hill.

Or maybe, the true winner of the Battle of Bunker Hill was everybody's nemesis, the fog of war.

General Artemus Ward, Colonel William Prescott, General Israel Putnam and Colonel John Stark

As we know, June 15, 1775, was the day that General Artemus Ward received orders from the Massachusetts Committee of Safety to build fortifications on Bunker Hill in Charlestown. In a short crucial time-span; General Artemus Ward successfully protected the American military headquarters in Cambridge, the Committee of Safety and the Provincial Congress of the new State of Massachusetts. He helped to stop the British cold on the Charlestown Peninsula. He listened to everyone and anyone who petitioned him with their urgent needs. He was resolute and helped plant the seeds of American liberty. General Artemus Ward was appointed by the Second Continental Congress as major general in the Continental Army. He was second only to General George Washington in rank.

For the American nation, nothing but acclamation and praise should accompany the name of Colonel William Prescott. His tremendous and steadfast leadership was second to none. In his small redoubt he remained calm in the face of battle. He was focused in his purpose and he did his best to pass on this undaunted determination to his men.

When General Israel Putnam arrived in Cambridge with his Connecticut troops, "Old Put" was returning to protect Massachusetts the land of his birth. During the Battle of Bunker Hill, General Putnam was seemingly everywhere at once. He led and commanded American troops under exacting conditions. General Israel Putnam was one of the four men first appointed as a major general in the Continental Army by the Second Continental Congress.

"Live free or die" are famous words attributed to Colonel John Stark. These words should remind every American of the fierce determination which the founding generation championed. Colonel John Stark was the embodiment of American military-leadership. Without Colonel Stark and his steadfast New Hampshire-troops; the British most likely would have completely routed the Americans early in the Battle of Bunker Hill and would have suffered much less themselves. The New Hampshire troops carried a fighting spirit which was second to none at the Battle of Bunker

Hill. The New Hampshire troops were led by one of the best American-officers. That officer was Colonel John Stark.

"Live free or die."

The British Generals

Lt. General Thomas Gage was the Military Governor of Quebec, Canada, from 1760 to 1763. General Gage was subsequently appointed British Commander-in-Chief of North America in 1763. He held this position until 1775. General Gage was appointed Military Governor of Massachusetts Bay in 1774. General Gage was ignominiously recalled from Massachusetts and returned to England after the debacle of the Battle of Bunker Hill. He subsequently retired from military service; however, he was called back to military service from 1781 to 1782, because of the French threat to invade Britain toward the end of the American Revolutionary War.

The Right Honorable Viscount Major General Sir William Howe became Commander-in-Chief of all British Military Forces in North America after Lt. General Thomas Gage returned to England in 1775. General Howe served in this capacity from 1775 to 1778. He was a member of Parliament from 1758 to 1780. He resigned his post and returned to England in 1778. In 1779, General William Howe successfully defended himself when he faced censure for his actions taken in America. He was knighted as a member of The Most Honorable Order of the Bath and was also a member of the Privy Council of the United Kingdom.

The Right Honorable Major General Sir Henry Clinton served as the Commander-in-Chief of all British Forces in North America from 1778 to 1782. He succeeded Major General William Howe. He was a member of Parliament from 1772 to 1784. After the siege of Boston, he commanded various campaigns in 1777 and 1778. Major General Sir Henry Clinton was knighted in The Most Honorable Order of the Bath in 1777. He returned to England from North America in 1782 prior to the Treaty of Paris. Major General Clinton was appointed Governor of Gibraltar in 1794, but he died in London before he could assume the post.

Major General John Burgoyne was one of the three British generals ordered to America to support General Thomas Gage during the siege of Boston. After the evacuation of Boston by the British in 1776; General Burgoyne commanded a small army and was defeated by the Americans in 1777, at the Battle of Saratoga. Major General "Gentleman" Johnny Burgoyne became a prisoner of war and marched to Boston. He returned to England and once there, he received a lot of criticism for his defeat and for the entry of France into the war. When General Burgoyne wasn't involved in foreign military-campaigns, he took to the pen as a dramatist. He wrote several plays in the late eighteenth-century. "Gentleman Johnny" was a member of Parliament from 1761 to 1792 and a member of the Privy Council of the United Kingdom.

Sir General Robert Pigot was a nobleman who served with distinction at the Battle of Bunker Hill. Subsequently seven-years later, General Pigot commanded British troops in Rhode Island in 1782. He was a member of Parliament from 1768 to 1772. He also held the position of Warden of the Mint from 1771 to 1796.

General Artemus Ward's Account of the Battle of Bunker Hill

The following is the recorded text in General Artemus Ward's orderly book. It's the only written documentation to the battle that he made. It contains the losses of the Americans as follows:

"June 17. The Battle of Charlestown was fought this day. Killed, one-hundred and fifteen; wounded, three-hundred and five; captured, thirty. Total four hundred and fifty."

The Siege of Boston continued in earnest. Occasionally, small skirmishes took place at both the Charlestown Neck and the Boston Neck.

The Americans enjoyed taunting the British with handbills. One very famous handbill gave the Redcoats lots to think about.

Prospect Hill
1. Seven dollars a month.
2. Fresh provisions and in plenty.
3. Health.
4. Freedom, ease, affluence, and a good farm.

Bunker Hill
1. Three pence a day.
2. Rotten salt pork.
3. The scurvy.
4. Slavery, beggary, and want.

The Public Relations Campaign

A little more than a month had passed when the Massachusetts Committee of Safety published and released a brief overview of the Battle of Bunker Hill. It is interesting to note, that it would be decades until the battle fought on June 17, 1775, was commonly and solely known as the Battle of Bunker Hill and not referred to by any other name.

Narrative of the Battle of Bunker Hill, Prepared by Order of the Massachusetts Committee of Safety

The following accounts of the Battle of Bunker Hill come from the well-respected and eminent-historian Richard Frothingham. These accounts are documented in his wonderful book, *History of the Siege of Boston,* published in 1849.

The Committee of Safety passed the following vote: July 6, 1775.

This Committee have, with great concern, considered the advantages our enemies will derive from General Gage's misrepresentations of the battle of Charlestown, unless counteracted by the truth of that day's transactions being fairly and honestly represented to our friends and others in Great Britain; therefore,

Resolved, That it be humbly recommended to the [Massachusetts State] Congress, now sitting in Watertown, to appoint a committee to draw up and transmit to Great Britain, as soon as possible, a fair, honest, and impartial account of the late battle of Charlestown, on the 17th ultimo, so that our friends, and others in that part of the world, may not be, in any degree, imposed upon by General Gage's misrepresentations of that day's transactions; and that there also be a standing committee for that purpose.

In compliance with this recommendation, the Provincial Congress, July 7 ordered the Committee of Safety to be a committee for this purpose, and also to be a standing committee for like purposes. This committee (11th) being exceedingly crowded with business," requested Rev. Dr. Cooper, Rev. Mr. Gardner, and the Rev. Mr. Peter Thacher, to draw up a true state of this action, as soon as might be, and lay it before them. The following was accordingly prepared.

In Committee of Safety, July 25, 1775

In obedience to the orders of the Congress, this committee have inquired into the premises, and, upon the best information obtained, find that the commanders of the New England Army had, about the 14th ult., received advice that General Gage had issued orders for a party of the troops under his command to post themselves on Bunker's Hill, a promontory just at the entrance of the peninsula at Charlestown, which orders were soon to be executed. Upon which it was determined, with the advice of this committee, to send a party, who might erect some fortifications upon said hill, and defeat this design of our enemies. Accordingly, on the 16th ult., orders were issued, that a detachment of 1,000 men should that evening march to Charlestown, and intrench upon that hill. Just before nine o'clock they left Cambridge, and proceeded to Breed's Hill, situated on the further part of the peninsula next to Boston, for, by some mistake, this hill was marked out for the intrenchment instead of the other. Many things being necessary to be done preparatory to the intrenchments being thrown up, (which could not be done before, lest the enemy should discover and defeat the design,) it was nearly twelve o'clock before the works were entered upon. They were then carried on with the utmost diligence and alacrity, so that by the dawn of the day they had thrown up a small redoubt about eight rods square. At this time a heavy fire began from the enemy's ships, a number of floating batteries, and from a fortification of the enemy's upon Copp's Hill in Boston. It was directly opposite to our little redoubt. An incessant shower of shot and bombs was rained by these upon our works, by which only one man fell. The provincials continued to labor indefatigably till they had thrown up a small breastwork, extending from the east side of the redoubt to the bottom of the hill, but were prevented completing it by the intolerable fire of the enemy.

Between twelve and one o'clock and number of boats and barges, filled with the regular troops from Boston, were observed approaching towards Charlestown; these troops landed at a place called Moreton's Point, situated a little to the eastward of our works. This brigade formed upon their landing, and stood thus formed till a second detachment arrived from Boston to join them; having sent out large flank guards, they marched towards our lines. At this instant smoke and flames were seen to arise from the town of Charlestown, which had been set on fire by the enemy, that the smoke might cover their attack upon our lines, and perhaps with a design to rout or destroy one or two regiments of provincials who had been posted in that town. If either of these was their design, they were disappointed, for the wind shifting on a sudden, carried the smoke another way, and the regiments were already removed.

The provincials, within their intrenchments, impatiently waited the attack of the enemy, and reserved their fire till they came within twelve rods, and then began a furious discharge of small arms. This fire arrested the enemy, which they for some time returned, without advancing a step, and then retreated in disorder, and with great precipitation, to the place of landing, and some of them sought refuge even within their boats. Here the officers were observed, by the spectators on the opposite shore to run down to them, using the most passionate gestures, and pushing the men forward with their swords. At length they were rallied, and marched up, with apparent reluctance, towards the intrenchment; the Americans again reserved their fire until the enemy came within five or ten rods, and a second time put the regulars to flight, who ran in great confusion towards their boats.

Similar and superior exertions were now necessarily made by the officers, which, notwithstanding the men discovered an almost insuperable reluctance to fighting in this case, were again successful. They formed once more, and having brought some cannon to bear in such a manner as to rake the inside of the breastwork from one end of it to the other, the provincials retreated within their little fort.

The ministerial army now made a decisive effort. The fire from the ships and batteries, as well as from the cannon in front of the army, was redoubled. The officers, in the rear of their army, were observed to goad the men forward with renewed exertions, and they attacked the redoubt on three sides at once. The breastwork on the outside of the fort was abandoned; the ammunition of the provincials was expended, and few of their arms were fixed with bayonets. Can it then be wondered that the word was given by the commander of the party to retreat? But this he delayed till the redoubt was half filled with regulars, and the provincials had kept the enemy at bay some time, confronting them with the butt ends of their muskets.

The retreat of this little handful of brave men would have been effectually cut off, had it not happened that the flanking party of the enemy, which was to have come upon the back of the redoubt, was checked by a party of the provincials, who fought with the utmost bravery, and kept them from advancing further than the beach; the engagement of these two parties was kept up with the utmost vigor; and it must be acknowledged that this party of the ministerial troops evidenced a courage worthy a better cause. All their efforts, however were insufficient to compel the provincials to retreat till their main body had left the hill. Perceiving this was done, they then gave ground, but with no more regularity than could be expected of troops who had no longer been under discipline, and many of whom had never before seen an engagement.

In the retreat the Americans had to pass over the neck which joins the peninsula of Charlestown to the main land. This neck was commanded by *HMS Glasgow,* a man-of-war, and two floating batteries, placed in such a manner as that their shot raked every part of it. The incessant fire kept up across this neck had, from the beginning of the engagement, prevented and considerable reinforcements from getting to the provincials on the hill, and it was feared it would cut off their retreat, but they retired over it with little or no loss.

With a ridiculous parade of triumph, the ministerial troops again took possession of the hill which had served as a retreat in flight from the battle of Concord. It was expected that they would prosecute the supposed advantage they had gained by marching immediately to Cambridge, which was distant but two miles, and which was not then in a state of defence. This they failed to do. The wonder excited by such conduct soon ceased when, by the best accounts from Boston, we are told that, of 3,000 men who marched out upon this expedition, no less than 1,500 (92 of which were commissioned officers) were killed or wounded; and about 1,200 of them were either killed or mortally wounded. Such slaughter was, perhaps, never before made upon British troops in the space of about an hour, during which the heat of the engagement lasted, by about 1,500 men, which were the most that were any time engaged on the American side.

The loss of the New England Army amounted, according to an exact return, to 145 killed and missing, and 304 wounded; 30 of the first were wounded and taken prisoners by the enemy. Among the dead was Major General Dr. Joseph Warren, a man whose memory will be endeared to his countrymen, and to the worthy in every part and age of the world, so long as virtue and valor shall be esteemed among mankind. The heroic Colonel Thomas Gardner, of Cambridge, has since died of his wounds; and the brave Lt. Colonel Moses Parker, of Chelmsford, who was wounded and taken prisoner, perished in Boston jail. These three, with Major Willard Moore and Major Andrew McClary, who nobly struggled in the cause of their country, were the only officers of distinction which we lost. Some officers of great worth, though inferior in rank, were killed, whom we deeply lament. But the officers and soldiers in general, who were wounded, are in a fair way of recovery. The town of Charlestown, the buildings of which were, in general large and elegant, and which contained effects belonging to the unhappy sufferers in Boston, to a very great amount, was entirely destroyed, and its chimneys and cellars now present a prospect to the American, exciting an indignation in their bosoms which nothing can appease but the sacrifice of those miscreants who have introduced horror, desolation, and havoc, into these once happy abodes of liberty, peace, and plenty.

Though the officers and soldiers of the ministerial army meanly exult in having gained this ground, yet they cannot but attest to the bravery of our troops, and acknowledge that the battles of Fontenoy and Minden, according to the numbers engaged, and the time the engagement continued, were not to be compared to this; and, indeed, the laurels of Minden were totally blasted in the battle of Charlestown. The ground purchased thus dearly by the British troops affords them no advantage against the American Army, now strongly entrenched on a neighboring eminence. The Continental troops, nobly animated from the justice of their cause, sternly urge to decide the contest by the sword; but we wish for no further effusion of blood, if the freedom and peace of America can be secured without it; but if it must be otherwise, we are determined to struggle. We disdain life without liberty.

Oh, Britons! Be wise for yourselves, before it is too late, and secure a commercial intercourse with the American colonies before it is forever lost; disarm your ministerial assassins, put an end to this unrighteous and unnatural war, and suffer not any rapacious despots to amuse you with unprofitable ideas of your right to tax and officer the colonies, till the most profitable and advantageous trade you have is irrecoverably lost. Be wise for yourselves, and the Americans will contribute to and rejoice in your prosperity.

J. Palmer, per order. (37)

With the outbreak of war, no reconciliation seemed possible especially after the Battle of Bunker Hill. But amazingly in the last second of the last hour, some of the American leadership in the Second Continental Congress still offered the Olive Branch Petition to King George III and the British Parliament. These mournful words would be sent across the ocean to friends and allies in London.

The attempt by the Massachusetts Committee of Safety to transmit a true and factual account of the Battle of Bunker Hill was very important. The Americans wanted to covey to the British people and to the rest of Europe the deliberate and shameful actions by their former government. The Massachusetts Committee of Safety legally spoke only on behalf of

Massachusetts, but also with the tacit approval from the people of New Hampshire, Connecticut and Rhode Island.

More Testimonials

A sworn testimony of the burning of Charlestown was given to James Otis. Otis was a Justice of the Peace for the State of Massachusetts. A witness named William Cockran testified. His testimony is as follows:

"In regard to what I know of the setting fire to Charlestown, on the 17th of June, is- I was on Copp's Hill, at the landing of the troops in Charlestown; and about one hour after the troops were landed, orders came down to set fire to the town, and soon after the carcass was discharged from the hill, which set fire to one of the old houses, just above the ferry-ways; from that the meeting-house and several other houses were set on fire by carcasses; and the houses at the eastern end of the town were set on fire by men landed out of the boats."

William Cockran *Middlesex ss., August 16, 1775*

"William Cockran personally appeared before me, the subscriber, and made solemn oath to the truth of the within deposition."

James Otis, A Justice of the Peace Massachusetts Bay, New England.

It was testimonies like William Cockran's that the Americans sent to Britain, with the hope to sway British public opinion against conducting a full-fledged war.

By 1775, American provocateur Arthur Lee of Virginia, was working in England as an operative for Massachusetts. This account was sent to London, with the following letter to Arthur Lee:

In Committee of Safety, Watertown, July 25, 1775

Sir, - The Committee of Safety, having been ordered by the honorable Provincial Congress of Massachusetts to draw up and transmit to Great Britain a fair and impartial account of the late battle of Charlestown, beg leave to enclose the same to you, desiring you to insert the same in the public papers, so that the European world may be convinced of the causeless and unexampled cruelty with which the British ministry have treated the innocent American colonies.

We are, sir, with great respect, Your most humble servant,

J. Palmer, per order.

To Arthur Lee, Esq., at London.

There is among the manuscripts of the American Antiquarian Society, at Worcester, a copy of this account, with the interlineations and corrections preserved. It contains passages not in the printed copy. It is enclosed in a paper having the following statement, without a date:

The following account was written by a person who was an eye-witness of the Battle of Bunker's Hill. Some of the circumstances the intervention of the hill prevented him from seeing, for he stood on the north side of the Mystic River. What facts he did not see himself were communicated to him from Colonel Prescott, (who commanded the provincials) and by other persons, who were personally conversant in the scenes which this narrative describes. It was drawn up within one fortnight after the seventeenth of June 1775, while events were recent in the minds of the actors; and it is now faithfully copied from the draught then made in a great hurry. This must serve as an excuse for those inaccuracies and embarrassments of the style, which would have been altered, had not the author felt himself obliged to give a copy of the account precisely as it was then written. It was transmitted by the Committee of Safety of Massachusetts to their friends in England, and may now, possibly, be in the hands of some person there. The author signs his name, which, though it may give no other celebrity to the account, will, he hopes, convince those who know him that the account is true; for he flatters himself that they, none of them, can believe him guilty of the baseness and wickedness of a falsehood.

Peter Thacher

(**Author's Note:** Peter Thacher's name has also been spelled as Peter Thatcher in other historical accounts.)

General Thomas Gage's Flowery Explanation of His Disaster

The politician residing within General Thomas Gage, tried his best to spin the British disaster that he created at the Battle of Bunker Hill. Not surprisingly, he wrote favorably about his generals and his ministerial troops. But his omissions are glaringly absent, along with his half-truths. General Gage attempts to make the Battle of Bunker Hill appear as if it was just a walk in the park, adjacent to an English garden. But what was an incompetent general supposed to do? The admission of his failure would never be shown the light of day by this man.

The following is General Gage's skillful letter to the Earl of Dartmouth explaining his version of the Battle of Bunker Hill.

Official Account of General Gage

Published In *The London Gazette.*

Whitehall, July 25, 1775

This morning, arrived Captain Chadds, of *HMS Cerebus*, with the following letter from the Honorable Lieutenant General Gage to the Earl of Dartmouth, one of his majesty's principal secretaries of state.

Copy of a letter from the Honorable Lieutenant General Gage to Lord William Legge, Earl of Dartmouth and Secretary of State for the Colonies and First Lord of Trade.

Dated Boston, June 25, 1775

My Lord,

I am to acquaint your lordship of an action that happened on the 17th instant between his majesty's troops and a large body of rebel forces.

An alarm was given at break of day, on the 17th instant, by a firing from the *HMS Lively* ship of war; and advice was soon afterwards received, that the rebels had broken ground, and were raising a battery on the heights of the peninsula of Charlestown, against the town of Boston. They were plainly seen at work, and, in a few hours, a battery of six guns played upon their works. Preparations were instantly made for landing a body of men to drive them off, and ten companies of the Grenadiers, then of light-infantry, with the 5th, 38th, 43rd, and 52nd battalions, with a proportion of field artillery, under the command of Major General Howe and Breveted Brigadier General Pigot, were embarked with great expedition, and landed on the peninsula without opposition, under the protection of some ships of war, armed vessels, and boats, by whose fire the rebels were kept within their works.

The troops formed as soon as landed; the light-infantry posted on the right, and the Grenadiers upon their left. The 5th and 38th battalions made a third line. The rebels upon the heights were perceived to be in great force, and strongly posted. A redoubt, thrown up on the 16th, at night, with other works, full of men, defended with cannon, and a large body posted in the houses of Charlestown, covered their right flank; and their center and left were covered by a breastwork, part of it cannon-proof, which reached from the left of the redoubt to the Mystic or Medford River.

This appearance of the rebels strength, and the large columns seen pouring in to their assistance, occasioned an application for the troops to be reinforced with some companies of light-infantry and Grenadiers, the 47th battalion, and the First Battalion of Royal Marines; the whole, when in conjunction, making a body of something above 2,000 men. These troops advanced, formed in two lines, and the attack began by a sharp cannonade from our field-pieces and howitzers, the lines advancing slowly, and frequently halting to give time for the artillery to fire. The light-infantry was directed to force the left point of the breastwork, to take the rebel line in flank, and the Grenadiers to attack in front, supported by the 5th and 52nd battalions. These orders were executed with perseverance, under a heavy fire from the vast numbers of the rebels; and, notwithstanding various impediments before the troops could reach the works, and though the left, under Brigadier General Pigot, who engaged also with the rebels at Charlestown, which, at a critical moment, was set on fire, the brigadier pursued his point, and carried the redoubt.

The rebels were then forced from other strongholds, and pursued till they were drove clear off the peninsula, leaving five pieces of cannon behind them.

The loss the rebels sustained must have been considerable, from the great numbers they carried off during the time of action, and buried in holes, since discovered, exclusive of what they suffered by the shipping and boats; near one-hundred were buried the day after, and thirty found wounded, in the field, three of which are since dead.

I enclose your lordship a return of the killed and wounded of his majesty's troops.

This action has shown the superiority of the king's troops, who, under every disadvantage, attacked and defeated above three times their own numbers, strongly posted, and covered by breastworks.

The conduct of Major General Howe was conspicuous on this occasion, and his example spirited the troops, in which Major General Clinton assisted, who followed the reinforcement. And, in justice to Brigadier General Pigot, I am to add, that the success of the day must, in great measure, be attributed to his firmness and gallantry.

Lieutenant Colonels Nesbit, Abercromby, and Clarke; Majors Butler, Williams, Bruce, Spendlove, Small, Mitchell, Pitcairn, and Short, exerted themselves remarkably; and the valor of the British officers and soldiers in general was at no time more conspicuous than in this action.

I have the honor to be, &c.,

Tho. Gage (38)

Lord William Legge, the Earl of Dartmouth, was an interesting choice for General Gage to write to and attempt to explain his version of the

Battle of Bunker Hill. Although a friend of General Gage, Lord Dartmouth was one of the few politicians who was still sympathetic to the American cause at the beginning of the war. Lord Dartmouth held onto the prospect of peace, until he ultimately turned against the Americans. He rejected the Olive Branch Petition sent to London by the Second Continental Congress. He resigned in November of 1775.

It's beguiling that not one word from General Gage was written regarding the fiasco on the Mystic River beach. The battle on the beach was simply a mindless slaughter that was allowed to occur until 96 Redcoats lay dead on the sand. The surviving Redcoats ran for their lives.

Early in the Battle of Bunker Hill there wasn't any glimpse of sharp cannonading from the British field-pieces and howitzers. General Gage seems to think that his land-based, big-guns were active. British twelve-pound cannonballs naturally didn't fit into British six-pound cannons. When the correct size cannonballs finally arrived from Boston, it was only then that his cannons began to fire. This took place late in the fighting. Finally, there is no mention in his letter of how the Redcoats broke and ran, not once, but twice on their attempted assault upon the redoubt. General Gage's letter was pure eighteenth-century spin on the calamitous battle which he helped to unleash.

General Thomas Gage did not participate in the Battle of Bunker Hill. He came out of his comfortable office only once to view the battle from across the water with his telescope. One can only wonder what he was witnessing and what he was thinking.

On October 10, 1775, the British Army in Boston witnessed General Thomas Gage perform his last official act in Massachusetts. He turned over his command to General William Howe. General Gage had been recalled to England. He sailed away that very day.

General Thomas Gage, the British general who was fond of the American colonies and the American people, had completely failed in his mission to prevent a war and gain a peaceful resolution. Because of his superiors in London, proud General Thomas Gage was doomed to failure as soon as he arrived in Boston.

Letter from Colonel William Prescott, Addressed to John Adams a Delegate to the Second Continental Congress

Camp at Cambridge, August 25, 1775

Sir,

I have received a line from my brother, which informs me of your desire of a particular account of the action at Charlestown. It is not in my power, at present, to give so minute an account as I should choose, being ordered to decamp and march to another situation.

On the 16th June, in the evening, I received orders to march to Breed's Hill in Charlestown, with a party of about one-thousand men, consisting of three-hundred of my own regiment, Colonel Bridge and Lt. Colonel James Brickett, with a detachment of theirs, and two-hundred Connecticut forces, Commanded by Captain Knowlton. We arrived at the spot, the lines were drawn by the engineer, and we began the intrenchment about twelve o'clock; and plying the work with all possible expedition till just before sun-rising, when the enemy began a very heavy cannonading and bombardment. In the interim, the engineer forsook me. Having thrown up a small redoubt, found it necessary to draw a line about twenty rods in length from the fort northerly, under a very warm fire from the enemy's artillery. About this time, the above field officers, being indisposed, could render me but little device, and the most of the men under their command deserted the party. The enemy continuing an incessant fire with their artillery, about two o'clock in the afternoon, on the seventeenth, the enemy began to land a north-easterly point from the fort, and I ordered the train, with two field-pieces, to go and oppose them, and the Connecticut forces to support them; but the train marched a different course, and I believe those sent to their support followed, I suppose to Bunker's Hill. Another party of the enemy landed and fired the town. There was a party of Hampshire, in conjunction with some other forces, lined a fence at the distance of three score rods back of the fort, partly to the north. About an hour after the enemy landed, they began to march to the attack in three columns. I commanded my Lt. Colonel Robinson and Major Woods, each with a detachment, to flank the enemy, who, I have reason to think, behaved with prudence and courage. I was now left with perhaps one-hundred and fifty men in the fort. The enemy advanced and fired very hotly on the fort, and meeting with a warm reception, there was a very smart firing on both sides. After a considerable time, finding our ammunition was almost spent, I commanded a cessation till the enemy advanced within thirty yards, when we gave them such a hot fire that they were obliged to retire nearly one-hundred and fifty before they could rally and come again to attack. Our ammunition being nearly exhausted, could keep up only a scattering fire. The enemy being numerous, surrounded our little fort, began to mount our lines and enter the fort with their bayonets. We was obliged to retreat through them, while they kept up as hot a fire as it was possible for them to make. We having very few bayonets, could make no resistance. We kept the fort about one hour and twenty minutes after the attack with small arms. This is nearly the state of facts, though imperfect and too general, which, if any ways satisfactory to you, will afford pleasure to your most obedient humble servant.

William Prescott (39)

(**Author's Note:** Colonel Prescott's reference to Breed's Hill and not Bunker Hill, is likely the first written account describing his orders to occupy the high ground of Charlestown.)

A Letter from William Tudor to John Adams, on June 26, 1775

William Tudor joined the Continental Army shortly after General George Washington took command of American troops in Cambridge. Tudor provided legal advice to General Washington. He held the rank of colonel. Tudor eventually became the Judge Advocate General of the Continental Army.

"The ministerial troops gained the hill, but were victorious losers. A few more such victories, and they are undone. I cannot think our retreat an unfortunate one. Such is the situation of that hill, that we could not have kept it, exposed to the mighty fire which our men must have received from the ships and batteries that command the whole eminence. Eight-hundred provincials bore the assault of two-thousand Regulars, and twice repulsed them; but the heroes were not supported, and could only retire. Our men were not used to cannon-balls, and they came so thick from the ships, floating batteries, that they were discouraged advancing. They have since been more use to them, and dare encounter them." (40)

The Olive Branch Petition

The following is the Olive Branch Petition sent to King George III and the British Parliament by the Second Continental Congress.

It was approved by the Second Continental Congress on July 5, 1775. Lord William Legge Earl of Dartmouth received it on August 24, 1775. One day earlier, the king had issued his Proclamation of Rebellion.

To the King's Most Excellent Majesty:

Most Excellent Sovereign:

We your Majesty's faithful subjects of the colonies of New Hampshire, Massachusetts Bay, Rhode Island and Providence plantations, Connecticut, New-York, New Jersey, Pennsylvania, the counties of New Castle, Kent, and Sussex on Delaware, Maryland, Virginia, North Carolina and South Carolina, in behalf of ourselves and the inhabitants of these colonies, who have deputed us to represent them in general Congress, entreat your Majesty's gracious attention to this our humble petition.

The union between our Mother Country and these colonies, and the energy of mild and just government, produced benefits so remarkably important, and afforded such an assurance of their permanency and increase, that the wonder and envy of other Nations were excited, while they beheld Great Britain rising to a power the most extraordinary the world had ever known.

Her rivals observing, that there was no probability of this happy connection being broken by civil dissentions, and apprehending its future effects, if left any longer undisturbed, resolved to prevent her receiving such continual and formidable accessions of wealth and strength, by checking the growth of these settlements from which they were to be derived.

In the prosecution of this attempt events so unfavorable to the design took place, that every friend to the interests of Great Britain and these colonies entertained pleasing and reasonable expectations of seeing an additional force and extension immediately given to the operations of the union hitherto experienced, by an enlargement of the dominions of the Crown, and the removal of ancient and warlike enemies to a greater distance.

At the conclusion therefore of the late war, the most glorious and advantageous that ever had been carried on by British arms, your loyal colonists having contributed to its success, by such repeated and strenuous exertions, as frequently procured them the distinguished approbation of your Majesty, of the late king, and of Parliament, doubted not but that they should be permitted with the rest of the empire, to share in the blessings of peace and the emoluments of victory and conquest. While these recent and honorable acknowledgments of their merits remained on record in the journals and acts of the august legislature the Parliament, undefaced by the imputation or even the suspicion of any offence, they were alarmed by a new system of Statutes and regulations adopted for the administration of the colonies, that filled their minds with the most painful fears and jealousies; and to their inexpressible astonishment perceived the dangers of a foreign quarrel quickly succeeded by domestic dangers, in their judgment of a more dreadful kind.

Nor were their anxieties alleviated by any tendency in this system to promote the welfare of the Mother Country. For 'tho its effects were more immediately felt by them, yet its influence appeared to be injurious to the commerce and prosperity of Great Britain.

We shall decline the ungrateful task of describing the irksome variety of artifices practiced by many of your Majesty's ministers, the delusive pretenses, fruitless terrors, and unavailing severities, that have from time to time been dealt out by them, in their attempts to execute this impolitic plan, or of tracing thro' a series of years past the progress of the unhappy differences between Great Britain and these colonies which have flowed from this fatal source.

Your Majesty's ministers persevering in their measures and proceeding to open hostilities for enforcing them, have compelled us to arm in our own defence, and have engaged us in a controversy so peculiarly abhorrent to the affection of your still faithful colonists, that when we consider whom we must oppose in this contest, and if it continues, what may be the consequences, our own particular misfortunes are accounted by us, only as parts of our distress.

Knowing, to what violent resentments and incurable animosities, civil discords are apt to exasperate and inflame the contending parties, we think ourselves required by indispensable obligations to Almighty God, to your Majesty, to our fellow subjects, and to ourselves, immediately to use all the means in our power not incompatible with our safety, for stopping the further effusion of blood, and for averting the impending calamities that threaten the British Empire.

Thus, called upon to address your Majesty on affairs of such moment to America, and probably to all your dominions, we are earnestly desirous of performing this office with the utmost deference for your Majesty; and we therefore pray, that your royal magnanimity and benevolence may make the most favorable construction of our expressions on so uncommon an occasion. Could we represent in their full force the sentiments that agitate the minds of us your dutiful subjects, we are persuaded, your Majesty would ascribe any seeming deviation from reverence, and our language, and even in our conduct, not to any reprehensible intention but to the impossibility of reconciling the usual appearances of respect with a just attention to our own preservation against those artful and cruel enemies, who abuse your royal confidence and authority for the purpose of effecting our destruction.

Attached to your Majesty's person, family and government with all the devotion that principle and affection can inspire, connected with Great Britain by the strongest ties that can unite societies, and deploring every event that tends in any degree to weaken them, we solemnly assure your Majesty, that we not only most ardently desire the former harmony between her and these colonies may be restored but that a concord may be established between them upon so firm a basis, as to perpetuate its blessings uninterrupted by any future dissentions to succeeding generations in both countries, and to transmit your Majesty's name to posterity adorned with that signal and lasting glory that has attended the memory of those illustrious personages, whose virtues and abilities have extricated states from dangerous convulsions, and by securing happiness to others, have erected the most noble and durable monuments to their own fame.

We beg leave further to assure your Majesty that notwithstanding the sufferings of your loyal colonists during the course of the present controversy, our breasts retain too tender a regard for the kingdom from which we derive our origin to request such a reconciliation as might in any manner be inconsistent with her dignity or her welfare. These, related as we are to her, honor and duty, as well as inclination induce us to support and advance; and the apprehensions that now oppress our hearts with unspeakable grief, being once removed, your Majesty will find your faithful subjects on this continent ready and willing at all times, as they ever have been with their lives and fortunes to assert and maintain the rights and interests of your Majesty and of our Mother Country.

We therefore beseech your Majesty, that your royal authority and influence may be graciously interposed to procure us relief [sic] from our afflicting fears and jealousies occasioned by the system before mentioned, and to settle peace through every part of your dominions, with all humility submitting to your Majesty's wise consideration, whether it may not be expedient for facilitating those important purposes, that your Majesty be pleased to direct some mode by which the united applications of your faithful colonists to the throne, in pursuance of their common councils, may be improved into a happy and permanent reconciliation; and that in the meantime measures be taken for preventing the further destruction of the lives of your Majesty's subjects; and that such statutes as more immediately distress any of your Majesty's colonies be repealed: For by such arrangements as your Majesty's wisdom can form for collecting the united sense of your American people, we are convinced, your Majesty would receive such satisfactory proofs of the disposition of the colonists towards their sovereign and the parent state, that the wished for opportunity would soon be restored to them, of evincing the sincerity of their professions by every testimony of devotion becoming the most dutiful subjects and the most affectionate colonists.

That your Majesty may enjoy a long and prosperous reign, and that your descendants may govern your dominions with honor to themselves and happiness to their subjects is our sincere and fervent prayer.

The Olive Branch Petition was the last attempt by the Americans to avoid war with the mother country. It failed miserably. King George III would have nothing to do with reconciliation and peace. We do not know if he read the petition or even received it. King George III was determined to have his war with the contumacious rabble of America.

Echoes of Bunker Hill in London Four Years Later in 1779

Four years after the Battle of Bunker Hill a number of British victories had taken place in the fledgling United States. Yet British commanders, General William Howe and later General Henry Clinton seemed at times reluctant to fight the decisive battle that was needed to ultimately defeat the Americans. Meanwhile, General George Washington and the Continental Army were doing all that they could to continue to be a viable army and eventually drive these foreign invaders out of the new nation.

Many criticisms of the Battle of Bunker Hill appeared in British journals. A letter published in the *London Chronicle* on August 3, 1779, is a prime example of how the Battle of Bunker Hill still managed to hinder the British war effort. The following text is one of a series of critical compositions on the conduct of General Howe. It was subsequently printed in pamphlet form.

Criticism on the Battle of Bunker Hill, Printed in the Family Newspaper, *The London Chronicle* August 3, 1779

To the Printer of *The London Chronicle*:

If the English general [Howe] had had his choice given him of the grounds upon which he should find his enemy, he could not have wished to place the rebels in a situation for more certain ruin than that in which they had placed themselves at Bunker Hill. And yet, from some fatality in our counsels, or father, perhaps, from the total absence of all timely counsel, what ought to have been destructive to them proved only so to the Royal Army.

Everyone knows that the ground on which stood Charlestown and Bunker's Hill was a peninsula. The isthmus which joined it to the continent used originally to be covered at high water; but, for the convenience of the inhabitants, had a causeway raised upon it, which answered all the purposes of a wharf for landing upon. And the land adjoining was firm, good ground, having formerly been an apple orchard.

Nothing can be more obvious, especially if the reader will look upon the plan, than that the army, by landing at the neck of the isthmus, must have entirely cut off the rebels' retreat, and not a man of them could have escaped.

The water in the Mystic River was deep enough for the gun boats and smaller vessels to lie very near to this causeway, to cover and protect the landing of our own army, and to prevent any further reinforcements being sent to the enemy, as well as to secure the retreat and reembarkation of our own army, if that could have become necessary.

The ambuscade which flanked our troops in their march up to Bunker's Hill, and did so much mischief, had by this means been avoided.

Instead of bottling up the rebels, by landing at the isthmus, which was the place the most commodious for the descent, and for beginning the attack, the general unhappily chose to land in the face of the rebel intrenchments, and at the greatest possible distance from the neck or isthmus, and thereby left the way open for their escape; and, still more unhappily, knowing nothing of the ground, attempted to march the troops in a part where they had ten or twelve rows of railing to clamber over; the lands between Charlestown and the beach being, for the convenience of the inhabitants, divided into narrow slips, not more than from ten to thirty rods over.

(**Author's Note:** Remember dear readers that only four years earlier in 1775; the plan of landing troops at the Charlestown Neck was presented by General Clinton at the Province House meeting on the morning of the battle. As we know, General Gage and General Howe both disregarded General Clinton's plan.)

The post and rails on the battlefield were too strong for the columns to push down and the march was so retarded by getting over them, that the next morning they were found studded with bullets, not a hand's breath from each other. This was well known to the inhabitants of Boston; but they thought that military men such a great English general as Mr. Howe, must know better than they. All this might have been known, and should have been known, to the English commander.

Had the rebels' coming into this peninsula been a thing utterly unexpected and never before thought of, the suddenness of the event might have been an apology for their not instantly thinking of the measures most proper to be taken upon such an occasion. But, far from unexpected, this was an event which they had long been apprehensive of, the possibility of which had been in contemplation for two months before. The action at Bunker's Hill was on the 17th of June; and so long before as the 21st of April, a message had been sent to the Selectmen of Charlestown, that if they suffered the rebels to take possession of their town, or to throw up any works to annoy the ships, the ships would fire upon them. The message giving them this warning doubtless was very proper. But it was easy to foresee, that if the rebels chose to possess themselves of any part of the peninsula, the inhabitants of Charlestown could not prevent it. In all these eight weeks, therefore, it might have been hoped that the general and admiral should have concerted the proper measures for them to take, in case the enemy should come thither. It might have been hoped that the admiral should have perfectly informed himself of the depth of water in the Mystic River, and how near at the several times of the tide the vessels could come to the causeway. We might have hoped that the general would have informed himself of every inch of ground in so small a peninsula; and have previously concerted what he ought to do, and where he ought to land, upon every appearance of an enemy. And yet we do not seem to have given ourselves the trouble of a single thought about viewing the ground, or of considering beforehand what would be the proper measures to be taken in case the enemy was discovered, at three o'clock, a Council of War was to be called, which might as well have been held a month before, and many hours more given to the rebels for carrying on their works and finishing their redoubt.

The map will show us that Charlestown Neck lies at the utmost passable distance from the rebel quarters at Cambridge and Boston Neck; so that the troops had every possible advantage in landing at the causeway, and not a single man of the rebels could have escaped.

Is it necessary for a gentleman to be a soldier to see this? Will not every man's common sense, upon viewing the map, be convinced of it?

Whether, after the rebels were fled, General Clinton's advice to pursue was right or not, may be made a doubt. But if, instead of having sacrificed the lives of a thousand brave men by the want of all previous concert, and never having surveyed the ground; if, instead of this negligence and inattention, we had shut up the whole rebel force in the peninsula, and destroyed and taken the whole army, there can be no doubt but that we might very easily have been dispersed; and the other provinces not having then openly joined them, we should have heard nothing more of the rebellion.

It was said at the time, I have heard, that we are unwilling to make the rebels desperate; but I hope no military man would offer to give such a reason. Veteran troops, long possessed with a very high sense of honor, like the old Spanish infantry at Rocroy, might possibly resolve to die in their ranks, and sell their lives as dearly as they could, though I know no instance in modern war of this Spanish obstinacy. But for regular British troops to be afraid of shutting up a rabble of irregular new-raised militia, that had never fired a gun, and had no honor to lose, lest they should fight too desperately for them, argues too great a degree of weakness to be supposed of any man fit to be trusted in the king's service. Happy had it been for Mr. Burgoyne if Mr. Gates had reasoned in this manner, and left the king's troops a way open for their escape, for fear of making them desperate. And yet Mr. Gates, when he lived with his father in the service of Charles Duke of Bolton, was never thought to possess an understanding superior to other men; and the letters of some of the most sensible and best-informed men among the rebels show, that they thought him scarce equal to the command.

But what was it we had to fear by this notion of making them desperate? The rebels could not but see the execution they had done upon the royal army in their march; and yet they ran away the instant our troops were got up to them: - was this their point of honor? Had they found themselves cut off from all possibility of retreat, by our army's landing at the isthmus, in all probability they would have instantly thrown down their arms and submitted. If they had not, they must then have come out of their intrenchments, and fought their way through our army to get to the isthmus; that is to say, we chose to land, and march up to their intrenchments, and fight under every possible disadvantage, for fear that by landing at the Neck we should have obliged them to come out of their intrenchments, and fight upon equal terms, or even upon what disadvantages the general should please to lay in their way. But the innumerable errors of that day, if they had been known in time, might have sufficiently convinced us how little was to be expected from an army so commanded.

T.P. (41)

(**Author's Note:** The author of this letter chose to remain somewhat anonymous and presenting only initials for identification. It's interesting to note that four years after the Battle of Bunker Hill, powerful and passionate-emotions still emanated from the British populace.)

The Authorities on the Battle of Bunker Hill

The following excerpts are from some of the authorities on the Battle of Bunker Hill. They are short, narrative accounts of the battle, which were compiled by Richard Frothingham. They were used by Frothingham as source material contained in his tremendous book, *History of the Siege of Boston, and of the Battles of Lexington, Concord, and Bunker Hill.* The accounts that I have selected all were written in 1775, some just days or weeks after the battle. There are differing accounts regarding who was in command for the Americans during the battle. These eyewitness accounts depended mostly upon the where the eyewitness came from and where the eyewitness was during the battle.

June 19. – Colonel John Stark, in a letter to the New Hampshire Congress, dated at Medford, says that the Americans intrenched on "Charlestown Hill," and that he went on order by General Artemus Ward.

June 20. – William Williams, in a letter dated Lebanon, Conn., June 20, 1775, ten o'clock at night, and sent to the Connecticut delegation in [Second Continental] Congress, says: "I received it that General Putnam commanded our troops, perhaps not in chief."

June 23. – Rev. Ezra Stiles, of Newport, records in his diary details he gathered from persons who obtained information from General Putnam in the camp, who stated, "That Putnam was not on Bunker Hill at the beginning, [of the battle] but soon repaired thither, and was in the heat of the action till towards night, when he went away to fetch across reinforcements; and, before he could return, our men began to retreat."

June 30. – Rev. John Martin related to President Stiles of Yale University an account of the battle, who recorded it in his diary, with a rude plan of the battle. He was in the hottest of it, and supplies much interesting detail. He states the Americans "took possession of Bunker Hill, under the command of Colonel Prescott;" that application to General Ward for aid "brought Colonel [General] Putnam and a large reinforcement about noon;" and that Putnam was deeply engaged with the enemy.

July 5. – A letter (British) from Boston gives a detail of the action. It was one of the "celebrated fugitive pieces" that occasioned the inquiry into the conduct of General Howe, and reprinted in *The Detail and Conduct of the American War*. It is an excellent British authority.

July 12. – A letter of Samuel Gray, dated Roxbury, July 12, gives interesting facts relative to the battle. It calls the place "Charlestown Hill," and states that two generals and the engineer were on the ground on the night of June 16, 1775, at the consultation as to the place to be fortified.

July 20. – In a letter addressed to Samuel Adams, dated "Watertown, July 20, 1775," J. Pitts writes, that no one appeared to have any command but Colonel Prescott, and that General Putnam was employed in collecting the men.

July 22. – Captain John Chester, who commanded a Connecticut company, wrote a letter on the battle, dated "Camp at Cambridge, July 22, 1775," and addressed to a clergyman. It gives first a general view of the battle, and then details his own agency in it. It is an excellent authority. He gives the fact that, after the British landed, General Putnam ordered all the Connecticut troops to march to oppose the enemy.

August 20. – The *British Annual Register* contains a narrative of the battle in which it is stated that Doctor Joseph Warren was the acting major general in command. Some of the narrative in the *British Annual Register* is attributed to John Clark, First Lt. of the Royal Marines. Clark claims he was in the Battle of Bunker Hill. In London he published *An Impartial and Authentic Narrative of the Battle on Bunker's Hill, near Charlestown, in New England*. He claims his account was collected and written on the spot. It gives Howe's speech to his army. It states that Doctor Warren was supposed to be the commander; and that General Putnam was about three miles distant and formed an ambuscade, with about 3,000 men. A second edition of this pamphlet was printed in 1775. (42)

(Author's Note: First Lt. John Clark's testimonial is most likely fraudulent. Clark was reported to have been in a military jail in Boston during the Battle of Bunker Hill. He was awaiting his return to England to be cashiered out of the British Army for drunkenness.)

Afterword

In the year 1823, the Bunker Hill Monument Association was created in order to build a tall beautiful-monument in remembrance of the American fight for liberty and freedom. Governor John Brooks was its first president. Fifty years later on June 17, 1825, the cornerstone of the monument was laid with an impressive-ceremony. The Bunker Hill Monument was finished and dedicated on July 23, 1842, more than 17 years after its construction had begun.

The beautiful and majestic Bunker Hill Monument was constructed on the hallowed ground where Colonel William Prescott's Redoubt once stood on June 17, 1775. The patriots who conceived of and built the Bunker Hill Monument were the same men who fought at the Battle of Bunker Hill. This small group of prestigious men wanted to leave a noble and lofty monument for posterity. Their outstanding and tremendous effort was successful. Today the Bunker Hill Monument in Charlestown, is one of the premier Revolutionary War memorials in the United States.

A Personal Story

As a young boy crossing over the Mystic River Bridge to Charlestown; the impressive Bunker Hill Monument commanded my attention. As I gazed at the beautiful monument, the allure and wonderment of this grandiose obelisk offered my imagination an unambiguous window into the Battle of Bunker Hill. It was inspiring. I conjured-up scenes from the battle. I recall experiencing a strong alluring-pull, combined with emotional feelings. But what were these unknown feelings that I harbored? I didn't know. I also recall the feeling of bemusement. This personal mystery stayed with me for many years until a genealogical chase finally gave me the answer. It was electrifying. It was wonderful news for me.

By the time of my Grandfather George Stockwell's birth in 1899, my family's involvement in revolutionary Boston was forgotten. Why? I'll never know why. Nobody in my family had ever offered any historical account to me. I can only surmise that nobody in my family knew anything about my family's revolutionary-past. It wasn't until 1989, that I discovered the integral part that my ancestors had played in revolutionary Boston and the beginning of the American Revolutionary War. My ancestors had participated in the struggle to forge a new nation!

I received my genealogical good-news while I was at my mother's home on High Street in Charlestown. She lived a mere 500 feet from Colonel Prescott's Redoubt. I had just received all of my ancestors names and what they were doing during the Siege of Boston. They were besieging and fighting the British! The reader may recall that my fourth great-grandfather, Ensign Daniel Pike fought at the Battle of Bunker Hill. He served in Colonel Ephraim Doolittle's Regiment that is documented by author Richard Frothingham. Everything finally made sense to me. My childhood feelings were finally validated on that day in 1989! I understood why I had those mysterious feelings as a child. I found that I had two fourth-great-grandfathers, Captain Daniel Stockwell Jr. and Ensign Daniel Pike, two fifth-great-grandfathers Daniel Stockwell Sr. and Timothy Warren and one sixth-great-grandfather, Oliver Appleton Jr., as well as my fourth-great uncle, Major Moses Stockwell, all who had fought the British during the Siege of Boston. My family's revolutionary past was clearly documented. I finally had a hidden part of myself emerge from history. Revolutionary Boston was in my blood. The questions that I had asked myself as a young boy, were finally and graciously answered. This wonderful personal-information has allowed me to revel in my ancestor's American Revolutionary War achievements!

It was an amazing day for me in 1989, as those mysterious childhood-feelings engulfed this lover of American Revolutionary War history. It was now very clear to me why I had those feelings so many years ago.

The Changing American Death Count of the Battle of Bunker Hill

The American death count from the Battle of Bunker Hill continued to rise as time passed. As previously stated in this book, General Artemus Ward's orderly book declared; **115 Americans** dead on the night of June 17, 1775. By July 27, 1775, Commanding General George Washington wrote to his brother and said that **138 Americans** had been killed. However, the Committee of Safety on July 25, 1775, had reported that the death count stood at **145 Americans**. Many years later in 1849, Richard Frothingham listed the death count as **140 Americans.** Frothingham's death count is presented in his classic book, *History of the Siege of Boston*. Subsequently, one more American death was recognized raising the count to **141 Americans** dead. This fluctuating death count remained at **141 Americans**, until the beautiful Memorial Bronze Tablets erected at the Training Field in Charlestown on June 17, 1889, proclaimed the total to be **153 Americans** dead.

After a long and exhausting research, I the author, unequivocally proclaim that there are three more American deaths that need to be recognized. This brings the total to **156 Americans** who died or were mortally wounded from participating and fighting for American freedom and liberty at the Battle of Bunker Hill.

Complete List of Names of the Men Who Were Killed or Mortally Wounded and Later Died at the Battle of Bunker Hill June 17, 1775

(**Author's Note:** The three names that consolidate the American death count are as follows:

William Kench, William Robinson (from Connecticut) and a militia-man listed as Unknown. This is an account according to *The New England Chronicle*: or, *The Essex Gazette* dated, **September 14, 1775**, from the Massachusetts Historical Society archives.)

There are two men listed in the archives named William Robinson, but only one appears on the Memorial Bronze Tablets. Both men named William Robinson coincidentally died in captivity.

Index of the Names of the 156 American Soldiers Killed or Mortally Wounded at the Battle of Bunker Hill, June 17, 1775.

Key:
■ Taken Prisoner by the British
♦ American Officers

1. Abbot, Philip
2. Adams, Isaac
3. Alexander, Jeduthan
4. Allen, Thomas
5. Ashbo, Samuel
6. Ayres, Stephen
7. Bacon, Josiah
8. Bailey, Samuel, Jr.
9. Baldwin, Capt. Isaac ♦
10. Barnard, Jonas
11. Barr, Aaron
12. Barrett, John
13. Bason, Caesar
14. Bate, Jonathan
15. Blood, Abraham
16. Blood, Ebenezer, Jr.
17. Blood, Joseph
18. Blood, Sgt. Nathan
19. Blyth, John
20. Boynton, Jacob
21. Boynton, James
22. Broderick, Joseph
23. Brooks, Josiah
24. Caldwell, Paul
25. Callahan, Daniel
26. Carleton, David
27. Carlton, George
28. Chamberlain, Benjamin
29. Chandler, Joseph
30. Cheeney, William
31. Childs, Ebenezer, Jr.
32. Clogston, Paul
33. Colbourn, Thomas
34. Cole, John
35. Collins, Thomas
36. Coneck, James
37. Corey, Chambers
38. Corless, Jesse
39. Cram, Asa
40. Cummings, Matthew
41. Dalton, Caleb
42. Davis, John

43. Dillon, John ■
44. Dodge, James ■
45. Dole, Benjamin
46. Doyl, Thomas*
47. Eastey, Benjamin
48. Eaton, John
49. Evans, Daniel
50. Evins, Timothy
51. Faills, Ebenezer
52. Fairbank, Comeing
53. Farewell, Joseph
54. Fassett, Lt. Amaziah ■ ♦
55. Fisk, Amasa ■
56. Fisk, Peter
57. Fisk, Wainwright
58. Foster, Stephen ■
59. Fowler, Cpl. Philip
60. Fox, Roger
61. French, William
62. Gardner, Col. Thomas ♦
63. Gibson, John
64. Gordon, John
65. Gray, Jonathan
66. Green, Lucas
67. Hadley, Jonathan
68. Haggitt, William
69. Haynes, Joshua
70. Heards, Samuel
71. Herrick, Ebenezer
72. Hibbard, Joseph
73. Hill, Cpl. Samuel
74. Hills, Parker
75. Hobart, Isaac
76. Hobart, Simon
77. Holt, Jesse
78. Howe, Jonas
79. Huntington, David
80. Hutchinson, James
81. Jenkins, Jonathan
82. Jennings, Lebbeus
83. Kemp, David ■
84. Kemp, Joseph

85. Kench, William ■
86. Laughton, Ebenezer
87. Lawrence, John
88. Looker, Jonas
89. Lord, John ■
90. Lovejoy, Jonathan
91. Lyon, Asahel
92. McClary, Maj. Andrew ♦
93. McCrillis, William
94. McGrath, Daniel ■
95. McIntosh, Archibald ■
96. Manuel, John
97. March, Ichabod
98. Meacham, Cpt. William ♦
99. Meads, John
100. Melvin, John
101. Memory, Daniel
102. Milliken, James ■
103. Minott, Joseph
104. Mitchell, William
105. Moore, Maj. Willard ♦
106. Nelson, Samuel
107. Nevers, Phineas ■
108. Nims, Sgt. Asahel
109. Parker, Lt. Col. Moses ■ ♦
110. Parker, Nathaniel
111. Parker, Robert
112. Parsons, William
113. Patton, James
114. Peers, Edmund
115. Phelps, Sgt. Robert, ■
116. Pigeon, Moses
117. Pike, Simeon
118. Pollard, Asa
119. Pool, Francis
120. Poor, Moses
121. Poor, Peter
122. Prescott, Sgt. Benjamin
123. Reed, Benjamin
124. Robbins, David
125. Robinson, William ■
126. Robinson, William ■

127. Ross, Benjamin ■
128. Rowlandson, Wilson
129. Russell, Jason
130. Russell, Samuel
131. Scott, David
132. Shannon, George
133. Shattuck, Jeremiah
134. Simmons, Joseph
135. Smith, Benjamin
136. Smith, Gershom
137. Spaulding, Lt. Joseph ♦
138. Stevens, Darius
139. Stevens, Oliver ■
140. Story, Jesse
141. Taylor, Joseph
142. Thessill, John

143. Walker, Cpt. Benjamin ■ ♦
144. Warren, Major General
    Dr. Joseph ♦
145. Warrin, William
146. West Lt. Benjamin ♦
147. Wheat, Thomas Jr.
148. Wheeler, Amos
149. Whitcomb, Isaac
150. Whitcomb, Joshua
151. Whitcomb, Peter
152. Whitemore, James
153. Wood, Benjamin
154. Wood, Oliver
155. Youngman, Ebenezer
156. Unknown ■

* Thomas Doyl deserted from the King's troops.

One-hundred-fifty-six Americans were killed or mortally wounded at the Battle of Bunker Hill. Eleven officers and 145 militiamen.

**Thirty American-prisoners were taken by the British.
Twenty died in captivity.**

Timothy Kettle, a young lad from Charlestown was initially held among the prisoners, but he is listed as dismissed by the British.
The American prisoners were held captive in Boston for several months.

**Ten Americans Were Taken Prisoner by the British on June 17, 1775.
These are the men who survived their captivity.**

1. Bigelow, Benjamin ■
2. Deland, John ■
3. William, Lt. Scott ■
4. Perkins, John ■
5. Frost, Jacob ■

6. Sessions, Daniel ■
7. Norton, Jonathan ■
8. Peck, Philip Johnson ■
9. Wilson, Benjamin ■
10. Sullivan, Lawrence ■

Index of the Names of Americans Killed, Wounded or Missing at the Battle of Lexington and Concord, April 19, 1775.

Key: Killed
* Killed by the First Fire of the Redcoats

Lexington
1. Robert Monroe*
2. Jonas Parker*
3. Samuel Hadley*
4. Jona Harrington Jr.*
5. Caleb Harrington*
6. Isaac Muzzy*
7. John Brown*
8. John Raymond
9. Nathaniel Wyman
10. Jedediah Munroe

Menotomy
11. Jason Russel
12. Jabez Wyman
13. Jason Winship

Sudbury
14. Deacon Josiah Haynes
15. Asahael Reed
16. Thomas Bent

Concord
17. Capt. James Miles

Bedford
18. Capt. Jonathan Wilson

Acton
19. Capt. Issac Davis
20. Mr. Hosmer
21. James Howard

Woburn
22. Azael Porter*
23. Daniel Thompson

Charlestown
24. James Miller
25. Edward Barber
(14-yearold noncombatant)

Brookline
26. Isaac Gardner Esq.

Cambridge
27. John Hicks
28. Moses Richardson
29. William Massey

Medford
30. Henry Putnam
31. William Holly

Lynn
32. Abenego Ramsdell
33. Daniel Townsend
34. William Flint
35. Thomas Hadley

Danvers
36. Henry Jacobs
37. Samuel Cook
38. Ebenezer Goldthwait
39. George Southwick
40. Benjamin Daland Jr.
41. Jotham Webb
42. Perley Putnam

Dedham
43. Elias Haven

Beverly
44. Reuben Kenyme

Needham
45. John Bacon
46. Nathaniel Chamberlain
47. Amos Mills
48. Elisha Mills
49. Jonathan Parker

Salem
50. Benjamin Pierce

138

Watertown
51. Joseph Coolidge

Wounded
Lexington
1. John Robbins
2. John Tidd
3. Solomon Peirce
4. Thomas Winship
5. Nathaniel Farmer
6. Joseph Comee
7. Ebenezer Munroe Jr.
8. Francis Brown
9. Prince Easterbrooks

Concord
10. Nathan Barrett
11. Jonas Brown
12. Charles Miles
13. George Minot
14. Able Prescott Jr.

Framingham
15. Daniel Hemenway

Bedford
16. Job Lane

Acton
17. Luther Blanchard

Woburn
18. George Reed
19. Jacob Bacon
20. Mr. Johnson

Medford
21. William Polly

Lynn
22. Joshua Feit
23. Timothy Munroe

Chelmsford
24. Oliver Barron
25. Aaron Chamberlain

Danvers
26. Nathan Putnam
27. Dennis Wallis

Dedham
28. Israel Everett

Beverly
29. Nathaniel Cleaves
30. William Dodge III
31. Samuel Woodbury

Menotomy
32. Capt. Samuel Whittemore

Needham
33. Eleazer Kingsbury
34. Mr. Tolman

Newton
35. Noah Wiswell

Stow
36. Daniel Conant

Sudbury
37. Joshua Haynes Jr.

Missing
Danvers
1. Joseph Bell

Lynn
2. Josiah Breed

Menotomy
3. Samuel Frost
4. Seth Russell

Roxbury
5. Elijah Seaver

A Long, Hot, Epic, Awesome-Day

A long, hot, epic, awesome-day had just begun when the
clock struck midnight local time

This late spring day was destined to be inflamed; various
kindling was being prepared

Early morning New England coastal-dew rested upon
the tall, uncut green grass bending leeward

The old town stood empty while many hundreds of men
gathered on the local hills behind it

The men on the hills were soon busy preparing themselves for this long, hot, epic, awesome-day

Men muffled the sounds of their pickaxes and shovels as
they dug through flowing green grass

Majestic ships were moored sleeping in the harbor, they
were floating quietly at their anchor

Across the calm, gleaming water of a once busy bay,
men quickly obeyed demanding orders

Silence had long since departed, it scurried away leaving
pandemonium to engulf all the men

By mid-morning, assignments were flowing, keeping
pace with events unfolding along the shore

Many hundreds of men stepped off skiffs planting their
last shoe prints along the narrow beach

Colored brilliantly, crimson-red rows of men were inter-
spersed by the scintillating hardened steel

Hundreds of yards away, home-spun brown and drab
colors were on the backs of laboring men

The long, hot, epic, awesome-day continued, the noontime hour quickly approached and faded

It faded directly into a sweltering New England mugginess rife with somber trepidation and fear

The long, hot, epic, awesome-day continued, crimson-red rows of men trampled the green grass

Men with home-spun brown and drab colored clothing dropped their tools and raised muskets

As a mother labors to birth a child, the men on the hills labored to give life to a nascent nation

Men opposite each other were now the audience and actors on this long, hot, epic, awesome-day

Events unfolded; men were unable to escape the momentous curtain being raised before them

Brave men in crimson-red jackets and brave men in home-spun brown with drab colors, engaged

Resolute men fought heroically on the flowing green grass on this long, hot, epic, awesome-day

The battle stood-down and men parted their ways, some parted their lives any fear since departed

The men in crimson-red, the men in home-spun brown with drab colors, would reflect eternally

The June 17, 1775 battle on the two hills, behind the old town, on a late New England spring day

The day that the Battle of Bunker Hill took place; it was a long, hot, epic, awesome-day

By Marc Stockwell-Moniz

Paul Revere and Billy Dawes Ride

Let me tell you about the night in '75,
It's all about Paul Revere and Billy Dawes' ride,
Off they went with two strong steeds,
The Regulars are out, so patriots take heed,
With quick, strong steps and scarlet coats,
Then across the Charles went Paul in his boat,
One by land and two by sea,
His Majesty's boys in Lexington by three?
And off went Billy through the Back-Bay,
The lesser known of the two heroes today,
The Charlestown road, Paul did take,
Through Medford and Metotomy for Adams' sake,
Dawes arrived first to warn the town,
The Regulars are coming, they are bound,
Along the road Paul met some foes,
Got captured awhile, so there he laid low,
But the hero broke free and off he fled,
I must make it to Hancock is what he said,
So early in the morning, Paul arrived,
To tell Adams and Hancock that they must hide,
Then the patriot men gathered on the green,
Standing tall to greet the British scene,
So off rode the duo in the middle of the night,
To help launch a nation's maiden flight,
So, for ever and ever, they'll ride again,
The all-night ride of America's men.

By Marc Stockwell-Moniz after Longfellow

About the Author

Author Marc Stockwell-Moniz is a fourteenth-generation American.
Marc was born in Cambridge, Massachusetts in 1954.
He was graduated from San Diego State in 1978 with a degree in journalism.
His ancestors were among the group of settlers who received
the charter from King Charles to establish the Massachusetts Bay Colony.
They founded Charlestown, Massachusetts in 1628.
Several of Marc's ancestors fought in the American Revolutionary War under
the command of General Artemus Ward and later General George Washington.
Marc is a member of the Bunker Hill Monument Association,
Sons of the American Revolution and the Sons of the Union Veterans.
He lives in San Diego County, Ca. with his family.

Marc is also the author of:

George Washington's Unsung Heroes
Seeds of American Liberty: Co-author Jack Alves
Prayers For Today and Tomorrow
Ode To The Five Hole

References

1. Boston Main Public Library Archives. Boston, Massachusetts
2. Jack Alves, Marc Stockwell-Moniz-pg. 9 *Seeds of American Liberty*
3. Richard Frothingham-pg. 44 *History of the Siege of Boston*
4. Marc Stockwell-Moniz-pg. 25 *George Washington's Unsung Heroes*
5. Jack Alves, Marc Stockwell-Moniz-pg. 13 *Seeds of American Liberty*
6. Edward Hale-pg. 75 *The Memorial History of Boston* Vol. 3 Chapter II
7. Jack Alves, Marc Stockwell-Moniz-pg. 23 *Seeds of American Liberty*
8. Richard Frothingham-pg. 93 *History of the Siege of Boston*
9. Jack Alves, Marc Stockwell-Moniz-pg. 25 *Seeds of American Liberty*
10. Richard Frothingham-pg. 114 *History of the Siege of Boston*
11. Ibid., pgs. 94-95
12. Ibid., pg. 94
13. Ibid., pg. 113
14. Ibid.
15. Ibid.
16. Ibid., pg. 122
17. Jack Alves, Marc Stockwell-Moniz-pg. 32 *Seeds of American Liberty*
18. Richard Frothingham-pg. 127 *History of the Siege of Boston*
19. Ibid., pgs. 130-131
20. Jack Alves, Marc Stockwell-Moniz-pgs. 37-38 *Seeds of American Liberty*
21. Ibid., pg. 38
22. Ibid.
23. Richard Frothingham-pg. 137 *History of the Siege of Boston*
24. Ibid., pg. 140
25. Ibid.
26. Ibid., pg. 203
27. Ibid., pg. 142
28. Ibid., pg. 145
29. Jack Alves, Marc Stockwell-Moniz-pg. 37 *Seeds of American Liberty*
30. Richard Frothingham-pg. 148 *History of the Siege of Boston*

31. Ibid., pg. 150

32. Ibid.

33. Ibid.

34. Ibid., pg. 393

35. Ibid., pgs. 192-193

36. Jack Alves, Marc Stockwell-Moniz-pg. 45 *Seeds of American Liberty*

37. Richard Frothingham-pgs. 382-384 *History of the Siege of Boston*

38. Ibid., pgs. 386-387

39. Ibid., pgs. 395-396

40. Ibid., pg. 396

41. Ibid., pgs. 398-401

42. Ibid., pgs. 372-375

Index

W

Made in the USA
Middletown, DE
18 May 2021